Light Love Life

From Clare to Winnie — April 15, 1991, San Diego

Elizabeth of the Trinity

# Light Love Life
*A Look at a Face and a Heart*

*Edited by:*
*Conrad De Meester O.C.D.*
*and the*
*Carmel of Dijon*

*Translation by:*
*Sr. Aletheia Kane O.C.D.*

*English Language Edition:*
*ICS Publications*
*2131 Lincoln Road, N.E.*
*Washington, D.C. 20002*

*Editorial Assistant:*
*Fr. John Sullivan O.C.D.*

## Abbreviations

All Elizabeth's texts are indicated according to the numbering of the documents found in the critical French edition of her *Complete Works* [Washington, ICS Publications, 1984, three volumes.] To facilitate the reading, a few minor textual changes have been introduced.

**L** = Letter
**D** = Diary
**P** = Poems
**PN** = Personal Notes
**LR** = Last Retreat
**HF** = Heaven in Faith
**GV** = Greatness of our Vocation
**CE** = Composition Exercise

S, followed by the number of the page, refers to *Souvenirs* (1909).
OP and AP, followed by the number of the paragraph, refer to the *Summarium* of the Cause of Beatification of Elizabeth.
RB, CE, EP, AGN, refer to the documents which will be found in a volume yet to be published: *Elizabeth of the Trinity: Words, Personal Annotations, and First Eyewitnesses* (PAT)

## Photographs

The photographs of Elizabeth are numbered from 1 to 70.
A, B or C after one of these numbers indicates a detail of that particular photograph.
The other photographs (except for the symbolic pictures) in this volume are numbered starting with 101.

## English language edition of the Complete Works

Volume I: (General Introduction, Major Spiritual Writings)
Volumes II and III: in preparation
(Washington: ICS Publications)

## Library of Congress Cataloging-in-Publication Data

Elizabeth of the Trinity, Sister, 1880-1906.
Light, Love, Life.

Translation of:
Je te cherche dès l'aurore.
1. Elizabeth of the Trinity, Sister, 1880-1906.
2. Nuns—France—Biography.
3. Elizabeth of the Trinity, Sister, 1880-1906—Iconography.
4. Spiritual life—Catholic authors.
I. De Meester, Conrad. II. Title.
BX4705.E44A3   1987     271'.971'024
[B]   86-15301
ISBN 0-935216-07-3

## Acknowledgements

**Foreword:**
Bishop Jean Balland
**Photographs:**
Raymond Hoornaert
and
André Fasquel
Thérèse Laureyns
François Garnier
Jacques Delaborde
René Truchot
Joris Hoorne
**Printing:**
Bertrand Hoste and Son,
Beernem-Bruges
**Lay-out:**
Johan Mahieu, Bruges
**Photo-engraving:**
Jean-Marie Cardinael
Datascan, Bruges

Printed by "De Windroos,"
Beernem, Belgium

# Foreword

*Sister Elizabeth of the Trinity is known throughout the world, at least if one is familiar with the Order of Carmel or the history of Christian spirituality.*

*However, I often experience, especially with young people, that it is not so simple to make her known as she really is, for herself.*

*In addition to her writings which are now all available, there is a treasure that has been carefully gathered and preserved in the archives of the Carmel of Dijon: seventy photographs. Thus, thanks to photography, it becomes possible to "present," to bring Elizabeth amazingly close to us, to all: A special pedagogical and pastoral device.*

*We see her in her times, in her family, her monastic Community. We see her in her brief existence showing a varied and yet remarkably identical face as a child, adolescent, nun, that face with its clear composed features, unified by her gaze.*

*In this face presented to us, let us not seek only to satisfy our curiosity. We all need signs. We need to see in order to approach the Invisible. Moreover, Elizabeth's gaze, almost always steady in the long poses needed by photography at that time, is an invitation. A gaze interiorized very early, that calls us, like an icon, to share a secret; a gaze offered to us that we may penetrate further with her.*

*She herself guides us along this way and makes these photographs come alive through well-chosen quotations from her diary, her letters, her poems, and her spiritual writings. Sometimes the photograph evokes and the text explains.*

*Other times the photograph captures and the text opens, invites, with all of it expressed in "dots," in the lively rhythm of the snapshots. These "dots" are close enough together to trace the marked linear curve of her destiny, and yet spaced far enough apart so as to leave room for our questions, for our thirst to know her better and to know our own spiritual itinerary.*

*Did Elizabeth, herself so avid for light, guess that these "traces of light" imprinted on the negative would make her more familiar to us? While doubtless posing for the photographer most often out of obedience, she nevertheless helps us to welcome better what she called "her mission," the luminous imprint of God in us: "I think that in Heaven my mission will be to draw souls by helping them to go out of themselves in order to cling to God by a wholly simple and loving movement, and to keep them in this great silence within which will allow God to communicate Himself to them and to transform them into Himself."*

*We thank the Carmel of Dijon and Father Conrad De Meester for sharing a family heritage that came to maturity in the cloister. By doing this, they follow in Elizabeth's footsteps and those of the Holy Father who proclaimed her blessed for the good of the whole Church. A daughter of France went to "find her heaven on earth in her dear solitude of Carmel where she was with God alone" and, having become "wholly teachable" by infinite Love, she is given back to the universal Church, transfigured, for all of us, by "light, by love and by life."*

**† Jean Balland**
**Bishop of Dijon**

# General Introduction

This album presents the face of someone who during her life had captured the attention of others by the richness and depth of her gaze, because she had let herself be captivated by the beauty of God.

The young musician, Elizabeth Catez, had not only learned from the great lover, Mary Magdalene, to attune her interior ear "to listen to Him who has so much to tell us" (L 164), but also to "turn the eyes of her heart" (L 324) toward the Master's face to learn there, as St. Paul says, "the knowledge of the glory of God shining on the face of Christ." This knowledge she also humbly asked for from the other Mary, the mother of Christ, "in the silence of prayer." (L 231)

"Jahweh, whoever looks on you is resplendent!" she loved to repeat in the version she had of psalm 33:6. (LR 17)

In Carmel she begged the Holy Spirit to let her become for Jesus "another humanity in which He may renew His whole Mystery" (PN 15) and to become for others "a sacrament of Christ" (PN 14) "which radiates Him and gives Him." (L 252)

While retaining this admirable humanity which characterized the young Elizabeth Catez, Elizabeth of the Trinity, such a spiritual Carmelite, concentrates her ideal and her life in the continuity of listening—"I want to spend my life in listening to You"—and the continuity of gaze: "Through all nights, all voids, all helplessness, I want to gaze on You always and remain in Your great light. O my beloved Star, fascinate me so that I may not be able to withdraw from your radiance." (PN 15)

There is nothing selfish in this word "gaze." She who loved Christ wished to live with "her eyes fixed on His" in order to "discover there the least sign and the least desire." (PN 13) The absolute gratuitousness which runs through her life from the beginning is astonishing!

The young artist does not attempt to identify the mystery which draws her to itself. She does not take possession of it but gives herself and loses herself. She does not seek herself in the sweetness of love and the gifts received, which she never dreamed of analyzing even when she recalls their abundance. She rejoices only in increasing the happiness and the glory of her beloved God. If she desires ardently to be transformed into Jesus, it is to delight the eyes of the Father when He recognizes in her the Son in whom He delights. (PN 15) Dazzled by the beauty of God, drawn to contemplation of his inexhaustible love, the great powers of admiration in this heart, at once tender and strong, artistic and passionate, are wholly absorbed in the encounter of the thrice-Holy God, without ever losing her adaptability and alertness when her gaze met the gaze of her brothers and sisters of this earth in the concreteness of daily life.

## As if her eyes had seen the invisible

It was during a party while she was dancing and having a good time that Mme. d'Avout noticed her expression and whispered to her, "Elizabeth, you are not here, you see God..." (AP 648) In her eyes "there shone an indefinable radiance," said Louise Demoulin, an adolescent of modest background whom Elizabeth prepared for her first communion. "Her wholly luminous gaze was completely filled with the Beyond," declared Mme. Angles, who depicts Elizabeth for us as having a "very happy disposition, very playful." (OP 402)

One of the friends of her youth whom she met innumerable times when she came each day to see her close friend and neighbor, Marie-Louise Hallo, was her brother, Charles Hallo, who does not spare the superlatives when he describes Elizabeth for us as "very simple and with a surprising frankness... much loved by her companions... very happy, an excellent musician... her sweetness was reflected in the extraordinary and luminous expression of her eyes... purity was reflected in her gaze." (AP 794-800) And Berthe de Massiac assures us that she herself overheard some young men say at a dance when they were looking over their possible future wives: "She is not for us, look at that expression!" (OP 334)

Françoise de Sourdon will paint a less mystical, more mischievous portrait of her older friend who will always have the affection of a mother for her: "She had a tremendous drive. Her black eyes shone... She played the piano delightfully and with exquisite feeling... One day she was playing Chopin's *Ballade in A minor*. Later, my father, an excellent musician, said, 'that evening that little one brought tears to our eyes.' I idolized her! We played hide and seek... There were always little parties, sometimes with about forty children... She loved children's dances very much. During Mary's month (May), we sat in the chairs closest to the exit so as to slip out more quickly... Scarcely had they closed the tabernacle when we pulled at her to go for a walk... She always got along well with everybody. She was very elegant and well-groomed; she had a sense of perfection: her clothing and hair styles were in perfect taste. She did not love the world but she was in it and seemed to enjoy herself. She had incomparable black eyes, too large a mouth, and her nose turned up a little too much. She was very mortified... and yet she accepted all that was given her. We had the best cook in Dijon—and when Francine made pies...!" (EP 4:2-9)

"Although she was not very pretty," Antoinette de Bobet tells us, "she had a look about her! And a smile! What I see still is that radiance, that look. I feared she could see into me too clearly." (EP 9:4)

"I can still see Elizabeth's ardent and profound expression when she was looking at the Blessed Sacrament," recalls Germaine de Gemeaux. (EP 8:2) Mme. Hallo confirms this: "Never will I forget her expression. One could not describe Elizabeth's face when she came back from holy communion." But she also reports the opinion of Abbé Sauvageot who prepared the little girl for her first communion: "With her temperament, Elizabeth Catez will be either an angel or a devil." And she adds that Elizabeth, "at a party seemed to be enjoying herself very much" and that she "liked to look nice, with even a touch of coquetry." (EP 3:1-10) Moreover, this is what we notice on seeing her beautiful blouses (which she made herself) and her carefully arranged hair. When the good Rolland aunts of Carlipa teased her about this:

"For a future Carmelite, we think you could be more simple," she answered them, doubtless with a big smile, "that before entering Carmel, St. Teresa acted the same way, and she wanted to imitate her in everything!"
But when a priest remarked to her that "Carmel was too austere an order for her health," the aunts also reported her reply: "Oh, well, then I'll die..." (RB 13:4)

Mme. Farrat, a neighbor of the Catez family, informs us that "just a few days before her entrance, Elizabeth went to buy some new gloves for her last outing," and she added, "She was spontaneously perfect; we could not help loving her; it was her expression!" (EP 6:3-8)

Everyone knew already that she prayed much, and they noticed she always forgot herself for others. Very few knew about her penances and privations, her desire to offer herself, even to the extent of suffering, for Christ and for the Church.

## How to convey this "Radiance": Mother Germaine's problem

"Her expression, like a seal, rested on us;" "she had a special expression; she acted like everyone else, but not in the way everyone else did," (EP 13:3 and 15:7) testified the extern sisters who welcomed the visitors to Carmel and who met Elizabeth there many times.
On August 2, 1902, after she had reached her twenty-first birthday, she came to live in their house for good.

"What struck me," said Sister Agnes, who had been so close to Elizabeth during her brief existence in Carmel, "was the expression in her eyes; it was so deep, so limpid, so embracing... How many times I sensed that God was in it!" (AGN 3:3) The sub-prioress, Marie of the Trinity, confirms: "Truly she carried God within her, He radiated from her whole being..."

And the prioress, Mother Germaine of Jesus (who, moreover, had never seen an angel!) affirmed without the least doubt: "If a celestial being would have appeared to me I truly do not know if I would have found in his expression more purity, more light, more divine radiance than I observed in the appearance and expression of Sister Elizabeth of the Trinity, who was perfectly calm and unconcerned with self."[1]

One can understand, then, the distress of Mother Germaine, this remarkable Carmelite and spiritual pedagogue, at not being able to find, after Elizabeth's premature death on November 9, 1906, any photograph of the Carmelite that truly conveyed the transparent countenance of one who in her eyes was before all else a "soul." She found defects in each photograph, due either to technical imperfections or to the poses which lasted several seconds and obliged one to remain motionless, thus stiffening the features and expression, freezing for a moment the flow of life.

At the beginning of this century, seventy years after Niepce's inventions in France, fifty years after the beginning of the industrialization of photography, it was still the adolescent little sister of the great lady, painting. On the canvas the portrait artist could patiently bring together, harmonize, accentuate, retouch and begin again as needed, the qualities of his client such as he saw them or as his client dreamed of having them. And, at that time, in the shadow of painting, a photographic "portrait" could still be retouched, embellished, touched up by one who had the ability for it, without the ordinary mortal being offended by it. At that period no one would have complained that Mother Germaine had recourse to a "montage" in order to bring out better—as she hoped—this "soul" of Elizabeth. In a Carmel with whom the Carmel of Dijon was friendly and exchanged letters and photographs there was a young religious who had died in the odor of sanctity. The case of her retouched photographs was sufficiently present to Mother Germaine's mind for her not to have any more scruples for her Elizabeth than the sisters of the little Thérèse of Lisieux had had for her.

Moreover, these changes did not alter the features of Elizabeth's face even though the first two photographs that appeared in the "Souvenirs" (biography of Elizabeth written by Mother Germaine), and in particular the second which was the "classic" for more than half a century, are montages. But in order to explain that we will have to go back a few steps.

## "Don't move!"

There are fifty negatives (known at this time) of Elizabeth Catez as a young girl. Some were taken at more solemn moments: baptism, confirmation, a little after first communion, the "adieu" before entering Carmel. Others attempted to "capture" happy gatherings at the time of a trip, a visit or vacations together. Sometimes they were the work of a professional (photograph 2: Ch. Poupat in Bourges; 3 and 4: Maison Kintz in Auxonne; 5: E. Chesnay in Dijon; 48, 49 and 50: J. Mazillier in Dijon). But most of the time they are the work of an amateur: a good amateur or an apprentice.

Life stops for a moment, the group gets in order, and then, invariably the command sounds: "Pay attention! Don't move!" Everyone "freezes." The duration of the pose: one, two, four, five seconds according to the type of camera and the light at the time. The immobilized group enters through the lens into the dark chamber and slowly the light engraves it on the glass plate or film. Too bad if the duration of the opening of the lens was not correctly measured with the intensity of the light or if anyone moved during the pose, for then everything would be overexposed, underexposed or blurred. Also, the camera or the plate should not be of inferior quality.

No sign of "divine radiance" in the first photographs of little Sabeth, the unruly imp! Bright, open, wide-awake, penetrating eyes which reflect—as in a mirror of the soul—a lively and choleric temperament; one who looks life squarely in the face. It is the look of one who knows what she wants and wants what she knows. Lips that do not easily yield their smile.

There is goodness of heart on the face of the little girl of eight, nine, ten. Joy fills the little one at her confirmation, dressed in the white gown of her first communion.
The little girl's mouth is partially opened, as if ready to tell her greatest secrets, and her gaze plunges into the distance—if not the infinite—for the first time in these photographs.

A dreamy gaze at thirteen, sixteen, as if the future was approaching too slowly. It is a look which reveals that the explosive side of her nature has been under control for a long time.

At eighteen, twenty, the gaze is often turned within, as if in secret dialogue, and yet alert enough to be present to the least sign from others. It is a luminous gaze reflecting kindness and fidelity; a gaze whose secret she will reveal in Letter 62: "I am sending you my photograph; while it was being taken I thought of Him, so it brings Him to you." (photograph 49 or 50)

Elizabeth's eyes give her face a great openness.
The face reflects the unity and strength of her whole being. It was a happy discovery for us each time when modern techniques highlighted with precision the secrets of an old plate or heightened the features of a faded old proof.

If we could have seen Elizabeth during her lifetime, we would have recognized better her joy and thoughtfulness, her attention to others and the happiness she radiated. For that was another defect of earlier poses: you had to be *serious*, as in painted portraits! If the length of the pose had not already extinguished the freshness and spontaneity of the smile and the warm little flame in the eyes, conventions still forbade smiling too much in a photograph, for then it would not be a good picture!
"We did not succeed in making her see that she was smiling too much and that this smile would disfigure her," wrote Sister Thérèse, a Carmelite of Dijon, when she sent the Carmel of Lisieux a photograph of the group in which Sister Appoline of the Heart of Mary can be seen with a big smile. (photograph 140 on page 72)

Before Elizabeth joins Sister Appoline in Carmel, let us recall an incident that Abbé Golmard, confessor of the three Catez women, relates. (EP 11,7 and OP 318)
He had heard it firsthand. Before the departure of her daughter for Carmel, Mme. Catez wanted to have an oil portrait made and she asked a travelling artist to do it. Completely captivated by his subject, whom he contemplated at leisure during the long pose, the artist suddenly went up and kissed Elizabeth. She, doubtless feeling that he was not being paid for that, was deeply indignant and ended the sitting on the spot!

## A camera at the convent

On August 2, 1901, when Elizabeth went to seek
the profound solitude of Carmel and a life wholly hidden
in God, she never would have dreamed that five years
and three months later the Carmel would possess
twenty negatives of her (known at this time), taken in
the following circumstances.

Her first photograph as a Carmelite—photograph 51,
the postulant with the determined chin—dates only three
days from her entrance, when group photographs were
being taken at the time of the foundation of the Carmel
of Paray-le-Monial.

Shortly before this, the brother of Sister Geneviève of the
Trinity had offered them a second-hand camera with all
the necessary accessories, and the prioress, Marie of Jesus
(Mercier), was broadminded enough to accept the gift.
The 13/18 chamber (see figure 1) required poses lasting 2
to 4 seconds depending on the light. It already had
technical imperfections but it would still provide good
service for more than half a century!

Around the time of each sister's profession a photograph
was taken (or more if the first did not come out)
to be given to the family and to be kept carefully in the
albums of the monastery. The plate was kept in Sister
Geneviève's archives.

There were still two other occasions which gave the
family and friends the opportunity to photograph the
Carmelite themselves. The first was the Clothing when
the postulant left the enclosure to embrace her family and
attend the first part of the ceremony with them.
In Elizabeth's case we have five negatives of poor quality.
(photographs 52-56)

The second occasion was when the novice left the
enclosure shortly before her Profession to be interviewed
by the Bishop's delegate who examined the earnestness
and liberty of choice of her definitive commitment.

Fig. 1

Afterwards, she could spend one or two hours with her family in the exterior quarters of Carmel. From this we have six negatives of Sister Elizabeth taken on the day of canonical examination, December 22, 1902.

Doubtless, the meeting with her mother and her sister was a tearful one. (Moreover, Guite has tears in her eyes and is holding her handkerchief in her hand: photograph 60 on page 91). In all probability this was the last time that these three could embrace each other before the Carmelite would disappear in the monastery to see her dear ones no more except from behind the parlor grilles.

Elizabeth also has swollen eyes: is it from weeping or rather from fatigue caused by the interior suffering and darkness that she was experiencing at that time? For the first—and last—time, she kissed Georges Chevignard, her brother-in-law of two months. A fervent amateur photographer, Georges would take four negatives, 57-60, which, unfortunately, are not clear.

To be sure of having a good picture of her Carmelite daughter, Mme. Catez also invited the photographer, Mazillier, to whom we owe photographs 61 and 62. In this hour of emotion and suffering, in the presence of the photographer, her family, some friends, and the Extern Sisters, who for this occasion had placed a black veil and her white mantle on her, Elizabeth does not seem at all at ease. Required to pose in a rather incongruous setting which the reader will see in its place (photograph 61, page 92), she must have hoped it would soon be over: her head is somewhat bowed, she is looking down, the expression on her face is closed, even stiff, without any sparkle. In the more sober setting of photograph 62 she is more self-possessed; the expression in her swollen eyes has nothing of the sublime: it is an "ordinary" Elizabeth, but her attitude is no less impressive. This photograph would have an exceptional history as we will see.

## The profession photographs

After the solemnity of her Veiling on the 21st of January, 1903, Elizabeth posed before Sister Geneviève's camera for the traditional "Profession" photograph, in the traditional place, the garden, and in the traditional attitude which recommends holding a religious object in the hand.

Photographs 63 and 64 (Elizabeth standing) are taken at the same time with the same traces of melting snow. But in photograph 64 Elizabeth blinked her eyes during the pose which gives her expression a veiled look; moreover, the whole negative is not clear: this could not be sent to the family.

And so a new pose was attempted on another day (for there is no more snow). The result of photograph 65 did not find favor in the eyes of the judges either: Elizabeth is not sitting erect. Mother Germaine said that she was leaning over too much. And she had forgotten, either after work or after the meal, to turn down her sleeves.

A new attempt on still another day! An infallible index verifies it: the scapular and the toque (the white coif around the head) were secured by a pin and each day it was adjusted a little differently: today the toque is not as low in relation to the seam of the scapular. She has her sleeves down and there is a small bandage on the index finger of her left hand, doubtless because of chilblains from that winter season in an unheated Carmel. Elizabeth is standing very straight, but this time the chemistry of the camera is at fault: the gelatin of the plate had stretched, thus forming lines across Elizabeth's left cheek which disfigured her face on this side. They would let the matter rest...

## In search of the ideal image

At the beginning of 1907, as soon as the project of a biography of Elizabeth began to take shape, they thought of illustrating it with a beautiful photograph.
In looking at the excellent results that photo-techniques make possible for us to obtain today from the old plates of the four "Profession photographs," it would be unjust to blame Mother Germaine for not having been pleased with the poor proofs of those days.

Mother Germaine's glance fell on the face in photograph 48. Elizabeth's face, resting against her sister's, has an expression of tenderness and communion; at the same time her eyes are open as if to welcome the infinite.
That the young girl did not have on the Carmelite habit was the least of her problems. As the ample habits of the nuns did not let show anything more than the face and a few fingers, it would suffice to fit the face in a Carmelite toque!

So Sister Geneviève took some pictures of Mother Germaine who turned her head to the right in order to facilitate the later work (see photograph 147, page 73).

The photographer Chesnay glued the face of the young Elizabeth into Mother Germaine's toque and at the same time enlarged her forehead somewhat so that her hair would not show; after a few other retouches the whole was rephotographed, and here we have her as a Carmelite! (figure 2)

Fig. 2

Then, to find a good photo-engraver! Mother Agnes of Lisieux had pointed out to them, after her experiences with the photographs of Thérèse, the difficulties they would meet with before obtaining a good printed reproduction: "One time, I had twelve negatives of half-tone engraving made at twenty-two francs each," she wrote on May 21, 1907, to Mother Germaine, "all of them were failures and could not be used."

In the Carmel of Angers with whom they were friendly, Sister Thérèse of the Child Jesus also struggled to "Carmelitize" the young Elizabeth, and Sister Agnes (of Dijon) encouraged her on the 6th of January 1908, in these words: "Your work has turned out surprisingly well in view of the difficulties that we know it contains, but it does not capture either the expression or the appearance of our little saint. I don't want to discourage you, my very dear sister, but I don't think you can succeed, and you should not continue.
Just think, we ourselves have been working on it for a year! But at last, blessed be God, we have succeeded! We have a perfect Sister Elizabeth; it is really true to life!" (AGN 5:3)

Or almost. For on the following April 22, Mother Germaine would have recourse to Sister Thérèse of Anger's ability while complaining "this holy child does not spare us difficulties in regard to her picture. The latest attempt of the photographer is still less satisfactory than the preceding ones. The head is erect, the shoulder down, but the expression of the face is lifeless. It is no longer our Elizabeth. What should we do? Obviously, the charm of her photograph depends partly on this bowed head which, when held erect, no longer has this expression of abandonment and sweet yet serious serenity which was truly the distinctive mark of this heavenly expression. When held erect her face loses this charm because of the accentuated features, and we no longer find Elizabeth always radiant in spite of her deep recollection."

It's better to leave well enough alone and one cannot wait indefinitely: "The question of photographs has now been decided so as not to delay any longer the prompt printing" (of the *Souvenirs*), wrote Sister Marie of the Heart of Jesus to the Carmelites of Angers on the 17th of November, 1908.

In figure 3 we see the heliogravure made at Dujardin, which adorned the first edition of the *Souvenirs...* "We do not recognize her there; nothing reminds us of our angelic Elizabeth," sighed Mother Germaine in a letter to the Carmel of Anderlecht, February 10, 1910.

And so to change the photograph!

This time the choice fell on photograph 49, "our new photograph in front of the chapel entrance." But Mother Germaine's letter to Mme. Catez, August 13, 1910, (in which she announced this good news), showed that they still had to wait: "Chesnay is still not finished with his retouches and, overwhelmed with work, has not yet sent this photograph back to us, so we will have to send it at another time. God grant that we can make a good reproduction of it in heliogravure."

Fig. 3

This time Mother Germaine would feel that her prayer had been fully answered! (See figure 4)

Chesnay obtained good results for the third edition of the *Souvenirs* in 1911, and Mother Germaine reported to the Carmel of Anderlecht on February 21st:
"The new picture of Sister Elizabeth, as a whole, is very pleasing; they tell us that it is already a whole sermon in itself. At any rate, in it we find our little sister really true to life in her religious demeanor and her modest and simple attitude." Chesnay's work would remain the "classic" photograph of Elizabeth for more than half a century. It would often accompany her famous prayer, "O my God, Trinity whom I adore."

To attain his objective, Chesnay replaced the "ordinary" face of photograph 62 by the (authentic) one of photograph 49 which fit perfectly into the toque! He blocked out the holy water font and the carpet, redesigned the flagstones, redid the neck of the scapular, blotted out the white veil of the novice showing from under the scapular. But the body and the face, although taken at two different times, are authentic.

Fig. 4

## Working toward the present edition

When we undertook the critical edition of the *Complete Works* of Elizabeth of the Trinity in 1978, it seemed obvious to us that the writings called for faces and gestures: an edition of all her photographs and a basic biography (this is still in process because of added research and the rich documentation).

Little by little the treasure of Elizabeth's photographs in the archives of the Carmel of Dijon has been considerably enriched, especially at the time of Guite's death in 1954 when the Chevignard family bequeathed to the Carmel all that concerned Sister Elizabeth of the Trinity.
Our recent research and inquiries of descendants of Elizbeth's former friends revealed still other photographs![2]

Without excluding the possibility that in the future still more will be discovered, our inventory has stopped with seventy photographs: fifty of the young girl[3] and twenty as a Carmelite. We are reproducing them all in this volume, often enlarging the faces or a detail.
Having learned from Mother Germaine's experience, we have not retouched the old proofs even if they bore marks of time: spots, scratches, cracking.
While sometimes reducing useless space in the original, we have always wished to respect the least detail which could help in identifying a place or a person.

A detail can help to better establish the chronology of the photographs: the vegetation of nature, the place and people they were visiting during their vacations — the dates of which we know from other sources — the clothes they are wearing (the young girls' dresses become progressively longer between the ages of thirteen and sixteen). And, obviously, we notice the faces and height of people, especially Elizabeth's, although the women and young girls of this period (men also in their own way) seem older than they are in reality, because of the styles and dark color of their clothing or their hairstyles and hats. Also priceless from this point of view

is the presence of Guite at her sister's side: when we are able to determine her age we have only to add two years and seven months for Elizabeth's.

Also, we have to sometimes trust oral tradition and the recollections of Guite's daughter, Elizabeth of Jesus, a Carmelite in the convent in which her aunt lived. With the help of Marie-Louise Hallo, whose chronological indications are sometimes erroneous or contradictory, an attempt at dating had already been made around 1963.

It was obvious that the members of Elizabeth's family should appear in this album as well as other close friends or this or that correspondent, and again, certain places where she had stayed.

Above all, we had to feel Elizabeth's presence in the Carmel where she pursued her search for God in her community. We arrived there just in time in 1978, for one year later the building was to be demolished and the community transferred to its new home on the hill of Flavignerot.

Several times our confrere, Raymond Hoornaert, Carmelite, who is an expert in photography, worked at the monastery on Boulevard Carnot. If the Dijon sun was almost always at fault, the art and technique of the photographer, his heart and patience, made up for it.

Assisted by Sister Madeleine of the Cross, official photographer of Carmel and heir of the camera and archives of Sister Geneviève, from which we drew sometimes, he reconstructed as much as possible the setting in Elizabeth's time.

If this pictorial description of Elizabeth's past was to have a scholarly rigor in the presentation of the photographs, although we did not adopt exactly a photo-archivist's point of view, we certainly did not want this album to be a dry dossier.

As if her mouth had opened in the photograph, we have let Elizabeth speak, have let her communicate a little of that invisible flame that was burning in her during the frozen poses.

Thus we will often find her own words or will read a testimony, a brief linking text, and everywhere captions to accompany the photographs. Artists have given us "symbolic" photographs which suggest the Beauty and the Infinite that Elizabeth loved so much.
It is as if we were viewing a "life in pictures."

In order not to burden the volume and break its tone, we will give the photographic dossier with its explanations in the documentary volume which will accompany the future biography.[4]

Let us repeat once again what a joy it was to work together on this project with the Carmelites of Dijon-Flavignerot; some were Marys, others extraordinary Marthas! How we thank them for having faithfully kept and enriched this iconographic treasure and for giving it now to the People of God for whom their elder sister lived and died.

It was also a joy to collaborate with all my Carmelite brothers and sisters, thanks to whom this album as a family homage to Blessed Elizabeth of the Trinity could appear simultaneously in seven languages: French, Italian, Spanish, Portuguese, German, English and Dutch.

Light, Love, Life... At the moment when her search was going to end in the definitive Encounter, Elizabeth of the Trinity repeats the essential: "In the evening of life love alone remains!"

**Conrad De Meester, Carmelite**

1. OP 84.
We have emphasized Mother Germaine's tendency to "angelize" Elizabeth in our General Introduction to the *Complete Works,* Volume I, p. 39.

2. With the Carmel of Dijon we warmly thank Professor Bernard Chevignard and all the Chevignard family, Mme. Annie Hallo (daughter of Charles Hallo), M. and Mme. de Jacquelot (daughter and son-in-law of Marie-Thérèse de Rostang) and all the Rostang family, Mlle. Elizabeth d'Arbeaumont (daughter of Anne-Marie d'Avout), M. and Mme. Henri de Champs (son and daughter-in-law of Yvonne de Gemeaux), M. Pierre de la Robertie (grandson of Mme. Gout de Bize), M. Jean Ambry (son of Marie-Louise Maurel), Sister Andrée, O.P. (daughter of Cecile Lignon), the Carmels of Angers, Paray, Clamart, Lisieux, the Visitation of Dijon and all those who contributed or looked for documents and information.

3. We nevertheless counted photograph 1, the Camp of Avor, as a single number. In reality there exist three other pictures that are very blurred in which one can see a small white bundle in Mme. Catez's arms. It is Elizabeth all wrapped up in her baptismal robe.

4. *Elizabeth of the Trinity. Sayings, Personal Annotations and the First Eyewitness Testimonies* (PAT).

God,
You are my God,
From dawn I seek you;
My soul thirsts for you;
My flesh longs for you,
Like earth arid and parched, without water.

I have contemplated you in the sanctuary,
I have seen your power and your glory.
Your love is worth more than life.
Your praise will be on my lips!

All my life I will bless you,
Lifting up my hands, I will call upon your Name.
I will be satisfied as by a feast,
Joyfully I will sing your praise.

In the night I remember you.
I spend hours speaking to you.
Yes, you have come to my aid:
I shout for joy in the shadow of your wings.
My soul clings to you,
Your right hand holds me up.

PSALM 63

# Born To The Sound of Bugles...

**1** *On Sunday morning, July 18, 1880, Elizabeth Catez was born in this military building at the Camp of Avor near Bourges, "a quite rustic barracks which I'd have been happy to live in," she would write later. (CE 22)*
*She was baptized on July 22, feast of St. Mary Magdalene. The photograph was taken in the garden around the end of July. After recovering from childbirth, Mme. Catez, in the center, holds her first daughter wearing her baptismal dress. On her right, Commandant Guémard with his son Gabriel, and Héloïse, the Catez' maid.*
*At her left, Mme. Guémard and the happy father, Captain Joseph Catez, who is already forty-eight; his wife will be thirty-four in a month.*
*In the background an orderly holds the captain's horse.*

**101** *The chapel of the military camp where Elizabeth was baptized.*
*On the left and the right can be seen the small houses of the military men.*

Baptism has marked you with the seal of the Holy Trinity!
(GV 9)

102

2

**102** *Elizabeth's future mother,
Marie Rolland at about twenty,
with her father, Raymond Rolland,
about fifty-five, retired Commandant
and tax collector at Saint-Hilaire (Aude),
and her mother, Joséphine Klein, about
forty-six. Marie is their only child.*

**2** *Elizabeth is about nine months old.
The photographer, Poupat of Bourges,
has retouched the child's pupils on
the negative to accentuate them.
A "very beautiful, very lively child,"
the proud mother would write. (RB 1:1)*

**103** *Marie Rolland at about thirty.*

103

# An Unruly Child

3

*Writing to her own mother, her mother said in regard to the twenty-one month old imp:*

*"Elizabeth is very conscious of your illness: she not only prays but she is teaching her doll how to pray; she has just very devoutly made her kneel..."*
*"She is a real devil; she is crawling and needs a fresh pair of pants every day..."*
*"Elizabeth's fine prattling will amuse you very much; she is a big chatterbox..."*

Her mother relates:

"At the age of one, her passionate and choleric temperament was already showing itself.
She was very advanced in speaking for her age.
She was only nineteen months old when I was summoned urgently to the South because my mother was seriously ill.
A mission was being preached during our stay there and was to close with a blessing of the children.
A Sister came to ask me if the little one had a doll that could be used as the little Jesus in the crib; it was to be dressed in a robe covered with golden stars and would be unrecognizable to the child's eyes.
I brought the little one to the ceremony. The child was distracted at first by the people who were arriving, but when the Curé announced the blessing from the pulpit, Elizabeth glanced at the crèche, recognized her doll and, in a fit of rage, her eyes furious, cried out: "Jeanette! Give me back my Jeanette!" Her nurse was obliged to carry her out in the midst of general amusement. This passionate and choleric temperament kept growing stronger..." (RB 1:2-3)

4

**3-4** *Elizabeth at about two with Jeanette, her doll.*
*She was photographed in Auxonne where Captain Catez was stationed from the beginning of May 1882.*

# My Dear Papa!

**5** *Little "Sabeth," photographed in Dijon (at Chesnay's), shortly before her fourth birthday. Beginning November 1882, Captain Catez was stationed in Dijon. There her little sister Marguerite, "Guite," would be born on February 20, 1883.*

5

5a

My dear Papa,
It is so kind of you to think
of my dolls.
A little crocheted bonnet
for my doll would make me
very happy.
I find the time long without
you and I send you a kiss.

Elizabeth
April 28 1885 (L 2)

104

**6** *An enlargement of a fragment
of a torn photograph.
Elizabeth seems to be five years old.
She has a mitten on her hand,
so it must be rather cold.
She is clasping a masculine hand.
Is it her father's?*

**104** *Captain Joseph Catez,
photographed in Bourges at Poupat's at
the same time as Elizabeth (photograph 2).
He was born on May 29, 1832, of a very
poor peasant family in northern France
(Aire-sur-la-Lys); he is fifty at this time.
He is wearing the Military Medal
(the smaller one) and the Cross of
the Legion of Honor which he received on
January 18, 1881. He would retire in
June 1885. Unfortunately, the family
happiness would not last very long.
One Sunday morning, October 2, 1887,
the fine Captain died unexpectedly,
struck down by a heart attack.
Elizabeth (then seven years and two
months old), would recall this tragic
hour ten years later.*

It was in my weak child's arms,
Those arms which caressed you so,
That your short agony lasted,
The last struggle of life!
And I tried to hold on to
This last sigh, so enduring!

October 2, 1897 (P 37)

# I Was Determined!

**7**  *Out for a walk.*
*The leaves are already falling: perhaps it is October 1887?*
*If so, it would be shortly after her father's death and Elizabeth—in the center of the photograph, at the top—would then be seven years and three months old.*
*Guite is seated on the table surrounded by unidentified persons.*

**8**  *Definitely the summer of 1888.*
*Elizabeth, carefully holding her little sister's hand, is eight.*

I had such a love for prayer, and for God, that even before my first communion, I could not understand how anyone could give their heart to another. From then on I was determined to love only Him, and to live only for Him.
(S 22-23)

Canon Angles reverently related: "She was endowed with a lively, ardent, passionate temperament.
She could easily have been quick-tempered, self-willed, impetuous, but happily, two loves were the steadying influence on her liveliness: love of her mother whom she cherished madly, and love of God whom she always called in a heavenly tone: Him!
Her large, beautiful eyes reflected Heaven.
I can still see her on our walks through the mountains, the woods, the meadows, crossing the rivers, always at the head of the group.

"One evening the two little girls, tired of playing, had begun a childish conversation. By a clever and smart move Elizabeth managed to climb up on my knees.
Quickly she leaned over and whispered into my ear: 'Monsieur Angles, I will be a religious; I want to be a religious!'
She was, I believe, seven…
I will always recall her mother's somewhat irritated exclamation: 'What is that little fool saying?'
Mme. Catez well knew where she could find me the next day. Anxiously she asked me if I seriously believed in her vocation.
And I answered, the words piercing her soul like a sword: 'I believe in it!'" (RB 5:3-4)

**105** The cloister of Saint-Hilaire, a former Benedictine abbey. The rectory door, in the center, faces this cloister.

**106** Canon Isidore Angles, who died in 1923 at eighty-five. From 1886 to 1897 he was pastor of Saint-Hilaire where Mme. Catez lived before her marriage and where the family often returned for the summer vacations. He became Elizabeth's close confidant.

106

105

**9-11**  *It is summer time.
Elizabeth appears to be nine.
According to Marie-Louise Hallo,
this group, and also the other
two photographs (as all the details
suggest), was taken at the camp
of Châlons-sur-Marne.
The house behind the group seems to be
a military barracks.
Elizabeth (seated) is the first one on
the right; Guite is the third.
Behind the children, the second one
to the right (standing) is Mme. Catez,
who is surrounded by unidentified
persons: the ladies are doubtless
the wives of military men.*

**107**  *The Dijon train station from which
the Catez family, frequent travelers,
often left.
The main building and the station
square are on the right.*

9

11

10

107

# Violence And Tenderness

*Concerning her sister's
childhood, Guite testified:
"She was very lively,
even quick-tempered!
She went into rages that
were quite terrible!
She was a real little devil!
Her rages in her early
childhood were sometimes
so violent that they threatened
to send her as a boarder
to the Good Shepherd
(a "house of correction"
nearby), and said they would
prepare her little bag."*

Dear Mama,
I want to wish you a happy
New Year and to promise you
that I will be very good,
very obedient, and I will never
make you angry with me again.
I will not cry any more and
I will be a good little girl so
as to make you very happy,
but you may not believe me.
I will do everything possible
to keep my promises so that I
will not have told a lie in my
letter as I have done sometimes.
I had a long, long letter in mind
but now I can't think of a thing!
Just the same you will see that
I will be very good.
I give you a kiss, dear Mama.

Your loving daughter,
Elizabeth Catez
January 1, 1889 (L 4)

10a

33

# This Great Day

12

**12** *Elizabeth—at the left—is ten;*
*she is still wearing pendant earrings,*
*different from the small round ones*
*that can be seen after her*
*first communion and which must*
*have been given to her that day.*
*Mme. Catez, a widow, is only forty-four*
*but, as the result of a snakebite which*
*altered her complexion and her features,*
*she seems much older.*

**108-109** *Saint-Michel (exterior and*
*interior), the parish church*
*where Elizabeth made her first*
*communion on April 19, 1891.*
*She wept for joy.*
*As she was leaving the church and*
*going down the steps she said to*
*her little friend, Marie-Louise Hallo:*
*"I am not hungry, Jesus has fed me..."*

Cherished Mama,
if I love God a little,
it is you who directed the heart
of your little one toward Him.
You prepared me so well for
the first encounter, that big day
on which we gave ourselves to
each other completely!

September 6, 1903 (L 178)

108

109

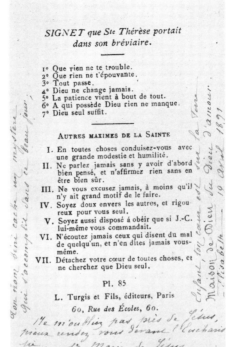

SIGNET que Ste Thérèse portait
dans son bréviaire.

1° Que rien ne te trouble.
2° Que rien ne t'épouvante.
3° Tout passe.
4° Dieu ne change jamais.
5° La patience vient à bout de tout.
6° A qui possède Dieu rien ne manque.
7° Dieu seul suffit.

AUTRES MAXIMES DE LA SAINTE

I. En toutes choses conduisez-vous avec
une grande modestie et humilité.
II. Ne parlez jamais sans y avoir d'abord
bien pensé, et n'affirmez rien sans en
être bien sûr.
III. Ne vous excusez jamais, à moins qu'il
n'y ait grand motif de le faire.
IV. Soyez doux envers les autres, et rigou-
reux pour vous seul.
V. Soyez aussi disposé à obéir que si J.-C.
lui-même vous commandait.
VI. N'écoutez jamais ceux qui disent du mal
de quelqu'un, et n'en dites jamais vous-
même.
VII. Détachez votre cœur de toutes choses, et
ne cherchez que Dieu seul.

Pl. 85

L. Turgis et Fils, éditeurs, Paris
60, Rue des Écoles, 60.

110

**13-14**  *Photographs 13 and 14 (page 36)
are certainly not taken on April 19,
the day of her first communion.
In Dijon the roses—a beautiful one can
be seen above Elizabeth's head—do not
bloom before May!
First communicants don their white dress
again for the sacrament of confirmation:
Elizabeth's was on June 8th at the church
of Notre-Dame.
Doubtless the photographs date from this
happy day and are taken in the garden
of the house on Rue Prieur de la Côte d'Or.
Elizabeth is almost eleven.
Her white-gloved hands hold the
beautiful* Roman Hand Missal
*with gilt edges and the initials "E.C."
engraved in gold on the cover.
A beautiful blue rosary with
a silver cross hangs from her right
wrist and on the left wrist is
a chaplet of matching beads.
She is wearing a mother-of-pearl
cross and a gold medal of
the Virgin Mary.*

**110**  *This picture was given her
for her first communion by the Prioress
of Carmel, Mother Marie of Jesus,
whom the communicants could go visit
on that day. On it she wrote the meaning
of the name "Elizabeth": "House of God."*

**111**  *Above the ancient Dijon houses
rises the tower of the church of Notre-
Dame where Elizabeth was confirmed.*

111

# First Communion, April 19, 1891
# Confirmation, June 8, 1891

14

*Seven years after her first*
*communion, Sabeth recalls*
*"this great day" in Poem 47:*

...That day
When Jesus made His dwelling within me,
When God took possession of my heart
So completely and so well that since that hour,
Since that mysterious colloquy,
That divine, delightful converse,
I have aspired only to give my life,
To return a little of His great love
To the Beloved of the Eucharist
Who rests in my poor heart,
Inundating it with all His favors.

April 19, 1898 (P 47)

# Sabeth

**15**  *From left to right, Mme. Catez, Guite, and Sabeth, with two unidentified persons. Elizabeth has on the same dress as in photograph 12 but she is wearing the new earrings, a gift for her first communion. On her left wrist is the little chaplet which she wore for the photographs taken then. So it is most probably after April 19, 1891.*

**15a**  *Elizabeth*

# Music! And Still More Music!

**16** *On July 24, 1893, Elizabeth, despite her young age—she became thirteen a week previously—won first prize for piano at the Conservatory of Dijon. The photograph was taken at the beginning of August in the Gemeaux chateau.*

16

*Except for lessons at the Conservatory, Elizabeth did not attend school.*
*Mlle. Irma Forey gave her lessons in general education and the arts at her home.*
*This education turned out to be rather incomplete.*
*As for music, she had been studying at the Conservatory since she was eight, and every day spent many hours at the piano at home.*
*Often she actively participated in concerts organized in the city by the Conservatory and the main Theater of Dijon which was quite close to Saint-Michel. Her precocious mastery would win for her the praises of the local newspapers.*
*In 1894, at the Conservatory, she would be unjustly deprived of the Prize for Excellence.*
*She recounts the incident with dignity:*

I have been so busy with the competitive examinations...
There was great excitement at the Conservatory because of me: the board had unanimously awarded me a prize but M. Fritsch, whose pupil had also previously won one, felt that I would tarnish the glory of his pupil; he ran to the prefecture, so did Mme. Vendeur. They succeeded so well that the prefect sided with them and said that the board did not have the right to give this prize. Then the members of the board, very upset, wanted to resign, and if M. Deroye, the president of the board, had been notified, things would not have turned out as they did, for he would have gone to find the prefect: he told M. Lévèque so...
In short, it caused an excitement you cannot imagine. And M. Fritsch was the cause of it all; a fine way to act!
He is annoyed with M. Diétrich. Marguerite won second prize at piano; this is superb.

Beginning of August 1894 (L 7)

**112** *M. Adolphe Diétrich. Elizabeth's major professor. He dedicated this photograph in 1897 to "his excellent pupil."*

**113** *Mme. Valentine Vendeur.*

112

113

# Vacation

**17-20**  *August 1893.*
*On vacation in Gemeaux (Côte d'Or),*
*at Mme. de Sourdon's.*
*Her daughters are: Marie-Louise*
*(the taller) and Françoise (the shorter one).*

I am delighted with my vacation.
We spent two weeks at Gemeaux with Madame de Sourdon who did not want to let us go.
We had a very enjoyable time there: we played endless games of croquet, took nice walks, and I often played the piano; Monsieur de Gemeaux loves music very much.
We often went to the chateau.

September 20, 1893 (L 6)

17

18

19

20

It was just before my
fourteenth birthday when one
day, during my thanksgiving,
I felt irresistibly impelled to
choose Jesus as my only spouse,
and without delay I bound
myself to Him by a vow of
virginity. We didn't say
anything to each other, but we
gave ourselves to each other
with such an intense love that
the determination to be wholly
His became for me more final
still.
(S 23)

19a

Jesus, my soul desires You,
I want to be Your bride soon.
With You I want to suffer—
And to find You, die.

August 17, 1894 (P 4)

# Physical And Moral Portrait

**114-115** *No family was as close
to them as the Hallos.
Elizabeth went there almost every day.
Marie-Louise, here at fifteen,
was a month younger than Elizabeth;
Charles was a year and a half younger.
It is for her "little brother" that the dying
Elizabeth will dictate the last phrase of
her last letter: "Elizabeth will love you
even more in heaven!" (L 342)
This did not prevent her, in the
meantime, from arguing with him one
day in Champagnole!*

**21**  *August 1895.
On vacation in Champagnole (Jura).
Behind Elizabeth are Mme. Hallo and
her son Charles (standing).
Seated on her right are Marie-Louise
Hallo and Guite. Mme. Catez, not in the
picture, is probably the photographer.
Elizabeth relates: "Everyday we set out
as tourists, either by carriage or on foot,
for we all have excellent legs and
20 kilometers do not frighten us." (CE 30)*

To draw one's physical and moral portrait is a delicate subject to
deal with, but taking my courage in both hands I set to work and begin!
Without pride I think I can say that my overall appearance is not
displeasing. I am a brunette and, they say, rather tall for my age.
I have sparkling black eyes and my thick eyebrows give me a
severe look. The rest of my person is insignificant. My "dainty"
feet could win for me the nickname of Elizabeth of the Big Feet,
like Queen Bertha! And there you have my physical portrait!
As for my moral portrait, I would say that I have a rather good
character. I am cheerful and, I must confess, somewhat
scatterbrained. I have a good heart. I am by nature coquettish.
"One should be a little that way," so they say. I am not lazy:
I know "work makes us happy." Without being a model of
patience, I usually know how to control myself. I do not hold
grudges. So much for my moral portrait. I have my defects and,
alas, few good qualities! I hope to acquire them!
Well, at last this bothersome task is finished and am I glad!"

End of November 1894 (CE 16)

# Carlipa, How Beautiful It Was...

We spent our morning on the beach admiring the sea, which I love so, and watching the bathers. At four we went to Carlipa where we were pampered and coddled by my cousins and we did honor to the excellent southern cooking.

August 10, 1896 (L 9)

*From Carmel Elizabeth would write her aunts:*

Didn't you feel my soul in this dear little church where, morning and evening, I so loved to come pray beside you? Do you also recall our walks on the Serre in the evening by the moonlight when we heard the lovely carillon?
Oh, how beautiful it was, my dear aunt, that starlit valley, that immensity, that infinity: it all spoke to me of God. Never will I forget those vacations spent with you; they will always be in my fondest memories...

Beginning of October 1902 (L 139)

**116**  *Every other year the Catez family stayed in Carlipa (Aude) with the mother's cousins whom Elizabeth called "aunt": on the left, Mathilde Rolland, who was hard of hearing, and her sister Francine, who could not see well, photographed in 1902 with their mother, "Aunt" Catherine (seated).*

**117**  *Right side-chapel of the little church of Carlipa. The white marble altar and the terracotta statue of the Blessed Virgin were donated by the Rolland family and faithfully decorated with flowers by the aunts. The harmonium Elizabeth played can be seen.*

**118**  *The village of Carlipa seen from the "Serre." The belfry of the church is visible. On a clear day it has as a backdrop the splendid Pyrenees mountain range.*

**119**  *Father Tescou, pastor of Carlipa for 57 years!*

**22-24** *Elizabeth at sixteen.*
*In 1896 in Limoux (Aude), the Catez were*
*guests of the Soujeole family.*
*The person in the middle cannot*
*be identified with certitude.*

At Saint-Hilaire they gave us
such feasts that our stomachs
were begging for mercy!
We are having a fine time
at Limoux. I have found my
dear friend, Gabrielle Montpellier,
again; she is twenty and a
charming girl. I am playing a
lot of music here. My friend
has an excellent baby grand
which is my delight:
it has a superb tone and I could
spend hours at it. I accompany
Gabrielle's cousin who plays
the violin very well.
Her husband is an excellent
pianist and we sightread music
for four hands.

September 22, 1896 (L 11)

23

22

24

# And What No One Sees...

22a

For my heart is always with Him,
Day and night it thinks unceasingly
Of its heavenly and divine Friend,
To whom it wants to prove its affection.

Also within it arises this desire:
Not to die, but to suffer long,
To suffer for God, to give Him its life
While praying for poor sinners.

December 8, 1897 (P 43)

# The Company Is Very Pleasant!

**25** *July 1898.*
*The house of the Rostang family in Tarbes.*
*Elizabeth is on the second floor, on the*
*left in the right window.*

**26** *Elizabeth at eighteen.*
*With the Rostang family.*
*From left to right: seated on the floor,*
*Solange and Raoul de Rostang;*
*behind the table, Mme. Catez and*
*Mme. de Rostang; standing,*
*Marie-Thérèse de Rostang, Guite,*
*Elizabeth, her dear friend Yvonne,*
*and Christine de Rostang.*

**27** *September 1898*
*In St. Hilaire with the Lignon family.*

25

We are having a very pleasant
time in Lunéville; breakfasting
with some, lunching and dining
with others, besides playing
tennis often with some very
nice girls...

July 19, 1897 (L 13)

27

26

Our stay here has been
a continual round of pleasures:
dances, musical sessions,
outings in the country,
all one after the other.
The company we keep in
Tarbes is very pleasant...
We do not leave the piano,
and the music stores of Tarbes
cannot keep us supplied with
enough music to sightread...
Day before yesterday was my
eighteenth birthday.
Madame de Rostang gave me a
lovely turquoise brooch...
I stop now to close
the trunks.
I will think of you at Lourdes.
From there we will travel
through the Pyrenees, Luchon,
Cauterets, etc.
I so love these mountains
which I contemplate while
writing you; it seems to me
that I cannot live without them!

July 21, 1898 (L 14)

**28**  *Still in St. Hilaire.*
*From left to right:*
*Guite, an unidentified young girl,*
*Mme. Catez, Mme. Lignon, Elizabeth and,*
*in the center, little Cecile Lignon.*

**29**  *Summer 1898.*
*According to Marie-Louise Hallo,*
*this group picture was taken in Auriac*
*(near Mouthoumet in Aude)*
*"at Mme. Brézet's home with the young*
*ladies of Crépy and Araille."*

**29a**  *Guite.*

29a

# Pentecost

With your pure and burning flames,
Holy Spirit, deign to enkindle my soul;
Consume it with divine love,
O you whom I invoke each day!

Spirit of God, brilliant light,
You fill me with your favors,
You inundate me with your sweetness,
Burn, annihilate me completely!

You give me my vocation,
Oh, lead me then to this intimate,
Interior union, to this life
Wholly in God, which is my desire.

May my hope be in Jesus alone,
And while living in the midst of this world,
May I long for, may I see only Him,
Him, my Love, my divine Friend!

Holy Spirit, Goodness, supreme Beauty!
O you whom I adore, you whom I love!
Consume with your divine flames,
This body and this heart and this soul!
This bride of the Trinity
Who desires only to do your will!

May 29, 1898 (P 54)

We were in mute ecstasy at the sight of these beautiful mountains which I am crazy about and would have liked never to leave.

July 25, 1898 (L 15)

# I Never Heard Her Say Anything Bad...

**30**  *Visiting the Chervaus at Couternon (Côte d'Or). October 1898.*
*From left to right: Alice Chervau, Guite, Marie-Louise Hallo and Elizabeth.*

**31**  *Same day. From left to right: Elizabeth, Alice Chervau, Guite and Marie-Louise Hallo who is looking at the tip of her nose.*

31a

31b

30

*A friend testifies:*
*"I never heard her say anything bad about anyone, nor did I ever hear her say anything good that was untrue. She knew how to bring out the good in each one, yet did not deny their defects. Her tact matched her charity; likewise her leniency did not prevent her from being firm when it was necessary."*
*(S 24-25)*

31

# I Hear His Voice In The Depths Of My Heart...

32a

Oh! What three delightful days I have just spent!
In the evening I made a good half hour of adoration before
the Blessed Sacrament until the Divine Office at 8:00.
Who could describe the sweetness of this heart-to-heart encounter
in which one feels no longer on earth, and no longer sees
nor hears anything but God! God who speaks to the soul;
God who communicates to it such sweet things: God who asks it
to suffer! In short, Jesus, who desires a little love...

February 12, 1899 (D 8)

**32**  Winter 1898-99.
*Elizabeth—in a beautiful plaid blouse—
is the third from the right.
Guite is the first on the left.
Alice Chervau is on the extreme right.
The other friends are not identified.
The two young girls on either side of
Elizabeth seem to be sisters.*

**32a**  *(opposite page) Elizabeth.*

**33**  *Spring 1899.
Elizabeth will soon be nineteen.
Notice the hat!
Is this the "little photograph made by
a friend" of which Letter 24 speaks?*

Today I had the joy of offering my Jesus several sacrifices
regarding my predominant fault, but how much they cost me!
I recognize my weakness there. It seems to me that when I
receive an unjust remark, I feel my blood boiling in my veins
and my whole being resents it! But Jesus was with me.
I heard His voice in the depths of my heart and then I was ready
to endure everything for love of Him!

January 30, 1899 (D 1)

# My Heart Is Not Free

34 *Elizabeth and Guite around the middle of 1899. In November 1898 she wrote: "I am involved in many projects. I so love to sew! Marguerite and I are learning English. I work hard at it so that I will soon be able to babble this language of birds."* (L 19)

This morning Mama returned very late and was quite excited... Someone had spoken to her about a marriage offer for me, a superb match that I would never find again.
But how indifferent I am to this attractive proposal!
Ah, my heart is not at all free; I can no longer dispose of it for I have given it to the King of kings. I hear the voice of my Beloved in the depths of my heart: "If you follow Me you will have suffering, and the Cross. But also what joys, what sweetness I will make you taste in these tribulations. Do you feel enough love for your Jesus? I want your heart. I love it. I have chosen it for Me. Keep your heart for Me!"
"Yes, my Love, my Life, Beloved Spouse whom I adore, yes, be assured I am ready to follow You along this way of sacrifices. Oh, You want to show me all the thorns that I will find. Good Jesus, we will pass through them together; following You, and with You, I will be strong."

Good Friday, March 31, 1899
(D 124)

34

38

41

9

May my life be a continual
prayer, a long act of love.
May nothing distract me from
You, neither noise nor
diversions, nothing.
O my Master, I would so love to
live with You in silence.
But what I love above all is
to do Your will, and since You
want me to still remain in the
world, I submit with all my
heart for love of You.
I offer You the cell of my heart;
may it be Your little Bethany.
Come rest there; I love You so…

January 23, 1900 (PN 5)

**35-38** *Around January 1900.
(During Christmas vacation?)
The photographs are small and blurred.
The young people, well bundled up,
(and with the winter sun in their faces!)
are—from left to right in photograph 35
—Marie-Louise de Sourdon, cheerful
Charles Hallo who is wearing the sports
pants of photographs 126 and 127 and
has grown his first mustache,
Françoise de Sourdon, who herself
is taking a picture, Elizabeth, Marie-
Louise Hallo and Guite.*

**39-41** *Same period.
Seated: Alice Cherveau, Guite and
an unidentified friend.
Standing: Elizabeth and Marie-Louise
Hallo, who would leave around the end
of January 1900 to try the religious life.*

40

# This Solitary Mountain Which Is Calling

**120** *The exterior quarters of Carmel (outside the enclosure) and the façade of the chapel.*

**121** *Mother Marie of Jesus.*

**122** *Father Vallée.*

**123** *Chapel interior.*
*On the left, the choir grille of the Carmelites and the door to the "communion window" through which the priest gave Holy Communion. On the left at the top, a painting of Christ on the cross; next to it, the grille of the little "tribune" where Elizabeth would pray so often during her illness. In the middle, the painting of the Agony in the Garden.*

*With many tears Mme. Catez gave her consent, often reconsidered, for Elizabeth to prepare for her entrance to Carmel, located barely 200 meters from their home. The young girl went there regularly to see the prioress, Marie of Jesus. There she also met Father Vallée, prior of the Dominicans of Dijon, who would strongly encourage her. With all her heart Elizabeth awaited her twenty-first birthday; then she could climb this "solitary mountain which seems like a little corner of Heaven." (P 72)*

Near their grille is a painting
In which one sees the divine Lamb
On the sad evening of His agony
Watching and praying
for everyone. (...)

Like them I want to leave all,
I long to give You my life
And to share Your agony.
May I die crucified.

September 1897 (P 34)

# Last Vacation

42

44a

Tell dear Mme. Lignon that her little friend still loves her very much and that she does not forget the pleasant vacations at Saint-Hilaire, the joyous evenings, and the dancing... I recall, dearest Mama, while I was dancing with the others and playing quadrilles downstairs in the large drawing room, that I was haunted by this Carmel which attracts me so and where, one year later, I was to find so much happiness. What a mystery! Oh, do not regret having given me to Him. He willed it; and then, you well know that I am always all yours!

From Carmel, September 6, 1903 (L 178)

43

44

**42** *September 1900.*
*With Marie-Louise Maurel, her good and joyous friend of Labastide-Esparbairenque (Aude), whom we see here between Guite and Elizabeth (on the right).*
*The photograph is very blurred.*

**43** *September 1900.*
*One last time at St. Hilaire.*
*Seated: Elizabeth, Guite, Mme. Catez, quite aged, Mme. Lignon and her daughter Cécile.*
*Standing: M. Lignon and his son, Antoine.*

**44** *In the same place.*
*Elizabeth and Marguerite, still with a flower in their hair.*
*Marguerite's is a marguerite.*

**44a** *Elizabeth*

43a

If you only knew all that I suffer in seeing my poor Mama
become so distressed at the approach of my twenty-first birthday...
Her behavior is contradictory: one day she tells me one thing,
the next day it is just the opposite...
How hard it is to make those we love suffer, but it is for Him!
If He did not sustain me, at certain moments I wonder what
would become of me; but He is with me, and with Him
I can do everything.

December 1, 1900 (L 38)

Isn't it true that one never tires of gazing at this beautiful sea.
Do you recall the last time we saw it together on the Rock of the
Virgin at Biarritz? What wonderful hours I have spent there.
Those waves sweeping over the rocks were so beautiful.
My soul thrilled before such a magnificent sight!

From Carmel, November 1, 1902 (L 144)

# "Not A Trace Of Austerity"

**45**  *September 1900.*
*While they were staying at the Chesnel chateau in Cherves (Charente) with the Roffignac family, they spent one day at the chateau "Les Bergerons" (in Roullet) with Mme. Elizabeth de Montleau and her husband. Elizabeth Catez (standing, third from the right) is between her two hosts. Her mother is in front of her.*

**46**  *Fragment of a photograph. Sabeth and little Gaetan, son of the Montleaus.*

**47**  *At the Chesnel chateau. Guite, Elizabeth (on the right) and an unidentified friend.*

**124**  *The Chesnel chateau.*

*Manitin Auburtin testifies regarding this stay at the Chesnel chateau:*
*"Elizabeth had a rare and delightful talent as a pianist; she felt music deeply.*
*It seems to me that I can still hear her playing "Le chant du nautonier." She was very lively and endowed with great charm, not a trace of austerity; she enthusiastically took part in the diversions of our age..."*

I think nothing can distract us from Him when we act only for Him, always in His holy presence, under that divine gaze which penetrates the inmost depths of the soul. Even in the midst of the world we can listen to Him in the silence of a heart which wants to belong only to Him!

December 1, 1900 (L 38)

45

47

46

124

# Last Months Together

We went to buy the material for Marie-Louise at the
new shirtmaker's on the Rue de la Liberté; there was a nice
choice. Afterwards Mme. Hallo took us for a snack at the pastry
shop. After dinner Charles gave us a concert; we ran through
*The Barber of Seville.*
I will wait until you return to see about the hats.
Besides, they can be made so quickly in the Parisian styles that it
won't take me long. Have a good time!
The horse show is going on now; it seems that it is outstanding
this year...
Nothing new to relate except for Madeleine Eugster's marriage
to M. Marchal, the handsome lieutenant of the Dragoons...
Do you remember Cauvel, that accessory shop in Paris?
One of his daughters, who married the Brothers' cook a few
days ago, lives there; her husband, the famous chef, is dreadfully
fat; poor boy, it is sad at his age!

From her correspondence of Spring 1901 (L 46, 65, 66)

**125** *The "horse show" of June 1901
which Elizabeth speaks of; it took place
in the old "Velodrome" in Dijon Park.
The second young girl on the left,
in the light-colored dress, is Elizabeth's
friend, Anne-Marie d'Avout.*

**126** *Charles Hallo, around 1901.*

**127** *Charles Hallo, summer 1900.*

# I Must Leave

48

Soon I will answer Your call;
soon I will belong wholly to
You; soon I will have said
good-bye to all that I love.
Ah, the sacrifice is already
made, my heart is detached
from all things; it costs
it hardly anything when it is
for You.
But there is a sacrifice that
will be painful to my heart,
a sacrifice for which I ask
You to really sustain me:
it is my mother, my sister.
I am happy to have a real
sacrifice to offer You, for You
have filled me with gifts and I,
what have I brought You?
So little, and this little is again
Your gift. Ah, at least I give You
a heart that loves You, a heart
that desires only to share Your
sufferings, a heart that lives
only for You, that wants only
You, that after so many years
desires only to give itself
to You... I will be Your bride,
a humble and poor Carmelite,
one crucified like You...

Easter, April 2, 1899 (D 133)

*48   Guite and Elizabeth,*
*in elegant blouses.*
*Spring 1901 ?*
*The pose suggests a farewell photograph.*

**128** *This is photograph 49 (see following page), later colored in pastels by the photographer Mazillier of Dijon.*
*However, in coloring it he slightly altered the picture: in particular, when reddening the lips he enlarged the upper one considerably.*
*We see the gold of the earrings and the pink of the dress. From the signature at the base to the top of the hair-do this photograph is 34 cm. (13 1/3 in.) in height. It is kept in the archives of the Carmel of Dijon. Doubtless, Mme. Catez had it painted at the same time as photographs 48 and 50.*

**129** *The enclosure door of Carmel which Elizabeth would soon go through.*

It was on the eve of the First Friday of the month.
Faithful to her rendezvous at Gethsemane, Elizabeth had just spent part of the night in prayer, when her poor mother, unable to sleep, came to kneel beside her bed, freely mingling her tears with those of her daughter who did not try to hide her broken heart.
"Then why are you leaving me?" the mother said.
"Ah! My dear Mama, can I resist the voice of God who is calling me?

Holding out His arms to me, He tells me that He is unknown, outraged, neglected. Must I, too, abandon Him? I must leave..."
When the moment arrived for her to leave her home forever, Elizabeth knelt before her father's portrait and asked for his blessing.

Her mother's testimony
(S 76-77)

**49-50** *Two farewell photographs, made during the first days of June 1901. The poses are slightly different. Elizabeth is twenty years and ten months. She explains: "I am sending you my photograph; I was thinking of Him while it was taken so it will bring Him to you."* (L 62)

49

130

**130**  *View of the outer wall of Carmel which runs along Boulevard Carnot. On the left, the large gate which led to the garden of the exterior quarters and the chapel which can be seen jutting out above the wall.*

There, in the depths of my heart, in the Heaven of my soul,
I love to find Him, since He never leaves me.
"God in me, I in Him." Oh, that is my life!
Did I ever tell you what my name will be in Carmel:
"Marie-Elizabeth of the Trinity." I think this name indicates a
special vocation; isn't it beautiful?
I so love this mystery of the Holy Trinity; it is an abyss in which
I lose myself!

June 14, 1901 (L 62)

# Entrance In Carmel, August 2, 1901

# Postulant In Carmel

**51a** *Detail of a group (photograph 51, page 73).*
*Elizabeth is wearing the postulant's black cape and veil.*
*She has taken off her earrings.*
*The photograph was taken on August 5, 1901, three days after her entrance.*
*On the next day, in a letter accompanying the photographs of the different groups, a sister describes Elizabeth: "A postulant of three days... who will become a saint for she already has a remarkable disposition for it."*

51a

— What is your ideal of sanctity?
— To live by love.
— What is the most rapid way to attain it?
— To become very little, to surrender oneself irrevocably.

August 9, 1901 (PN 12)

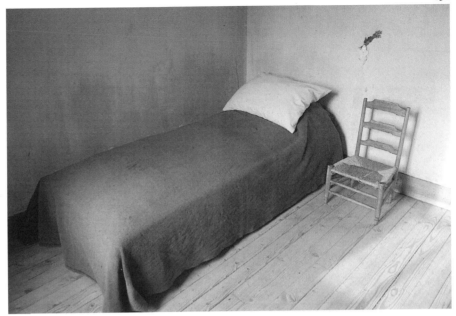

I sleep deeply on my straw mattress, something I never experienced before.
The first night I did not feel very secure and I thought that before morning I would roll out on one side or the other, but nothing happened, and now my bed seems delightful to me.
If you only knew how quickly time passes in Carmel, and yet it seems to me that I have always lived in this dear house.

August 22, 1901 (L 88)

I can't find words to express my happiness. Here, there is no longer anything but Him.
He is All; He suffices and we live by Him alone.
I find Him everywhere, while doing the wash as well as while praying. Just picture to yourself Elizabeth in her little cell which is so dear to her: it is our sanctuary, just for *Him* and for me...

September 11, 1901 (L 91)

**131** *Her cell window which looks out over the quadrangle.*
*At the right can be seen the corner of the infirmary.*

**132** *Elizabeth's cell.*
*Bed and chair.*
*It had no table; for writing they held a little wooden writing case on their knees. There was no running water, electricity or heat.*

# Food For The Body

**133** *The refectory, seen from the entrance.*
*The Carmelites took only two meals a day: at 10:15 A.M. and 6:05 P.M., always in silence, while a sister read from the pulpit which can be seen at the right. The prioress and the sub-prioress presided at the table in the back.*

**134** *A place-setting from Elizabeth's time. They did not yet use a fork.*

**135** *The refectory, seen from the presider's table. The pulpit is on the left. In the back on the left, a serving window through which the dishes from the kitchen were passed, then served by two sisters.*

To eat well, to sleep well, they say, are the conditions for making a good Carmelite; in that I leave nothing to be desired.
September 17, 1901 (L 94)

134

If I could just give you a little of my appetite: I devour my food; also they say that I look very healthy. Mme. d'Avout, who came to see me the other day, declared, on seeing me, that she was going to ask them to take Anne-Marie into Carmel in order to fatten her up! I eat everything, and the things that I could not swallow before now seem delicious to me.

September 12, 1901 (L 92)

133

135

# Food For The Soul

Every Sunday we have the Blessed Sacrament exposed in the oratory.
When I open the door and contemplate the divine Prisoner who has made me a prisoner in this dear Carmel, it seems to me rather like the gate of Heaven opening! Then I present to Jesus all those who are in my heart, and there, close to Him, I find them again. I do not regret these years of waiting: my happiness is so great it had to be paid for. Ask for me that holiness for which I so thirst.

September 11, 1901 (L 91)

**136-137** *Statues of the Virgin Mary and Saint Joseph on either side of the oratory altar.*

**138** *The oratory where, on Elizabeth's entrance day, First Friday of the month, the Blessed Sacrament was exposed, as also on all Sundays and Feast days. The altar was not always decorated with as many flowers as in this old photograph. The tabernacle, where the sisters adored the Blessed Sacrament behind the little grille that can be seen in the photograph, was built into the wall between the chapel and the oratory. After mass the priest came to place the monstrance there.*

**139** *The far end of the oratory. The entrance door of which Elizabeth spoke is on the left. Through the window one can see the quadrangle with its cloisters.*

# All My Sisters!

140

141

142

143

144

**140** *From left to right, seated: Appoline of the Heart of Mary (60), Aimée of Jesus (45); standing: Louise de Gonzague (36), Marie-Xavier of Jesus (53), Marie-Pia of the Immaculate Conception (52).
Between parentheses we have indicated the age of the sisters at the time of Elizabeth's entrance.
The groups date from summer 1901; photographs 141-143 from spring of 1900 or 1901.*

**141** *Ignace of Jesus (59).*

**142** *Marie of St. Bernard (39).*

**143** *Marie of the Heart of Jesus (56).*

**144** *The four sisters in the white veils were non-choir sisters who did not have the obligation of the choral office and performed the more domestic tasks.
From left to right, seated:
Marthe of Jesus (39), Marie of the Incarnation (71) who would die five days after Elizabeth, Anne-Marie of the Child Jesus (28); standing: Marie of the Holy Spirit (31) and Anne of Jesus (49).*

*From the 10th of October the Dijon community, which had just sent ten sisters (one of whom was the prioress, Marie of Jesus) to the new foundation of Paray-le-Monial, would number twenty including Elizabeth who was still a postulant.
We see the whole community here with the exception of Sister Marie of the Cross who was very ill and would die in January 1902.*

When the time approached for her to receive the religious habit, Mother Prioress said to her: "You still have much to acquire, perhaps it will be postponed."
Elizabeth answered: "It is true, my Mother, that I am quite imperfect, but I believe that God wants to do me this favor. As for my sisters, how can they refuse me?
They must love me for I love them so!"

Mother Germaine's testimony (S 94)

51

145

146

147

148

**51** *This photograph was taken August 5, 1901, on the terrace which leads to the infirmary; one can see the tall trees which were in the quadrangle at that time. From left to right, kneeling, Elizabeth of the Trinity (21), Mother Germaine of Jesus (31) who is holding in her hands the Story of a Soul* (autobiography of Sister Thérèse of the Child Jesus, Carmelite of Lisieux, who died four years before), *Geneviève of the Trinity (24), "official" photographer of Carmel; standing, Marie of the Trinity (26), the novice Hélène of Jesus (20) who would leave Carmel in June of the following year, and Agnes of Jesus and Mary (25).*

**145** *On October 9, 1901, Germaine of Jesus (standing) was elected prioress and would also assume the task of mistress of novices. Marie of the Trinity became sub-prioress. On the right, the former prioress, Marie of Jesus, who would leave the next day for Paray-le-Monial.*

**146-147** *Mother Germaine before her entrance, and in 1908.*

**148** *The recreation room. It was the only room (except the kitchen and the infirmary) which was heated; one can see the big cast iron stove. They spent an hour of recreation there at 11:00 A.M. and another at 6:40 P.M.: at this they spoke, sang, and laughed while at the same time doing some kind of work, at least during the week. The prioress and the older sisters sat on little benches; the others simply sat back on their heels on the floor! In summer they recreated in the garden.*

# Her Clothing

52    53    54    55    56

**52-56** *In the afternoon of Sunday, December 8, 1901, feast of the Immaculate Conception, Elizabeth received the Carmelite habit. The five photographs preserved, the work of an amateur, are unfortunately blurred or did not come out well. Wearing a very beautiful wedding dress of satin—white as on the day of her baptism, as on the day of her first communion—Elizabeth is surrounded by her family and her friends: first in the exterior quarters of Carmel where the photographs were taken, then in the chapel where the first part of the ceremony took place. According to certain witnesses, her joy was almost ecstatic.*

I am so happy to announce to you my immense joy.
On the 8th, this beautiful feast of her Immaculate Conception, Mary will clothe me in my dear Carmelite habit.
I will prepare myself for that beautiful day of betrothal by a three-day retreat. Pray much for your little Carmelite that she may be wholly surrendered, wholly given, and that she may give joy to her Master's Heart. On Sunday I would like to give Him something very nice, for I so love my Christ. The happy fiancée will finally give herself to Him who has been calling her for so long and who wants her to be all His.
Ask Him that I live no longer, but that He live in me.

December 1, 1901 (L 99)

# To Surrender To Love

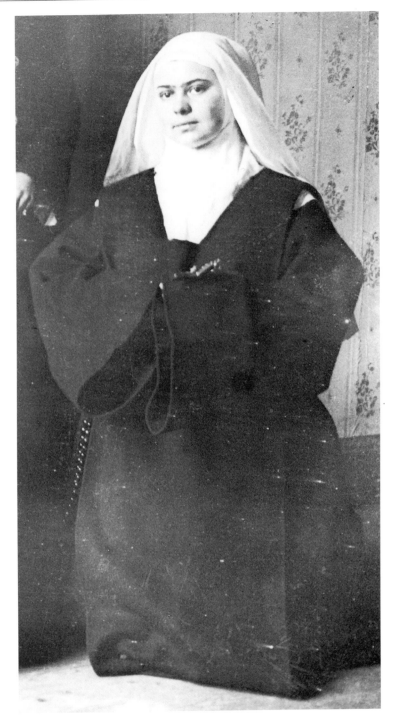

Oh, how good it is in silence
To listen to Him over and over,
To enjoy the peace of His presence,
and then to surrender wholly to His love.

O Lamb, so pure and so meek,
You my All, my only One;
How well You know that Your fiancée,
Your little one, hungers greatly for You.

She hungers to feed upon her Master,
Above all to be consumed by Him,
To surrender fully to Him her whole being
So she may be totally taken.

Oh, that I may be possessed by You;
One who lives by You alone,
Yours, Your living host,
Consumed by You on the Cross.

December 25, 1901 (P 75)

58a

**149** *The white mantles which the sisters wore for the Eucharist and more festive offices and occasions.*

**150** *The Choir.*
*Here the Carmelites attended the Eucharist which was celebrated daily in the chapel.*
*Through the grilles one can see the altar (on the left) and the side chapel of Our Lady of Mount Carmel (opposite).*
*The door on the left in choir opened onto the grille of the "communion window" through which the priest gave Holy Communion.*
*There, too, the sisters recited the choral office which was spread throughout the day and lasted in all around three and a half hours.*
*Kneeling or seated back on their heels, they also had an hour of silent prayer in the morning and an hour in the evening.*
*The choir was not heated!*
*The second choir bench on the left (starting from the chapel) was Elizabeth's.*

How good it is to unite with Heaven to sing the praises of God. It seems then that Heaven and earth are one and sing the same hymn. Oh! It is good to have God here so close, under the same roof!

August 30, 1901 (L 89)

I have such a love for the Divine Office!
Beginning of October 1902 (L 139)

149
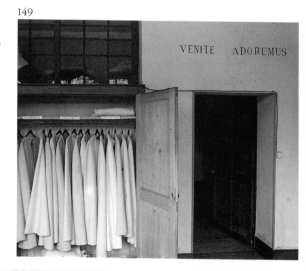

150

# When I See How He Gave Himself For Me...

You ask me how I can
endure the cold.
I suffered much more
from winter at home than I do
in Carmel where I have no heat
at all.
God gives the grace; besides it
is so helpful when I feel these
little things to look at the
Master who also endured all
that because He has "exceedingly
loved" us, as St. Paul says:
then I thirst to repay Him love
for love!
In Carmel I find many sacrifices
of this kind but they are so
sweet when the heart is wholly
taken by love.
I will tell you what I do when I
feel a little tired:
I look at the Crucified One and
when I see how *He* gave
Himself for *me*, it seems that *I*
can do no less for *Him* than to
spend myself, wear myself out,
in order to repay Him a little of
what He has given me!
In the morning, at holy Mass,
let us share in His spirit of
sacrifice...
Then, after that, let us always
stay in Him during the day...

February 15, 1903 (L 156)

**151-152**   *The far end of the choir,
(seen from the monastery side),
with the statue of Our Lady of Mount
Carmel (photograph 151) and a painting
representing, as in the outer chapel,
Christ's agony in the Garden of Olives.
In Elizabeth's time they had gaslight.*

**153** *The Large Cloister.*

The life of a Carmelite is a
communion with God from
morning to evening, and from
evening to morning.
If He did not fill our cells and
our cloisters, ah, how empty
they would be!
But through everything we see
Him for we bear Him within us,
and our life is an anticipated
Heaven.
I ask God to teach you all
these secrets.

June 19, 1902 (L 123)

153

Ah, If one could lift the curtain of Carmel, what a beautiful
horizon he would see on the other side! It is the Infinite, and that
is why it expands each day. Ah! this Carmel, this being alone with
Him whom we love...
I am doing quite well; Lent is not tiring me; I don't even notice it.
As for the cold, I would not know it was winter if I did not see the
beautiful curtains God has hung at our little window.
If you could see how lovely our cloister is with its frosted panes!

February 16, 1902 (L 109)

# I Looked And I Understood...

**154** *The quadrangle in Elizabeth's time. The next to last window in the left wing (marked by a small cross) is Elizabeth's cell.*
*"Our window looks out over the quadrangle, the inner garden surrounded by our large cloisters; in the middle on a rock a large cross stands out." (L 187)*

**155** *Elizabeth often prayed before this crucifix in the garden.*

154

155

A Carmelite is a soul who has gazed on the Crucified One;
who has seen Him offering Himself as a Victim to His Father for
souls and, recollecting herself in this great vision of the charity
of Christ, has understood the passionate love of His soul,
and has wanted to give herself as He did!
On the mountain of Carmel in silence, in solitude, in a prayer
that never ends—for it continues through everything—the
Carmelite already lives "with God alone" as in Heaven.
So she hungers for silence that she may always listen,
always penetrate further His infinite Being. She is identified with
Him whom she loves. She finds Him everywhere; through
everything she sees His radiance!
Is this not Heaven on earth!

August 7, 1902 (L 133)

# I Closed My Eyes...

*In the course of this year 1902, interior suffering visits Elizabeth.*
*She is in darkness, there are days of confusion, and at certain times anguish and agitation overwhelm her.*
*But she loves the Crucified-Risen One and gives herself blindly to Him.*
*Her writings speak of her happiness in believing in His love and in following Him.*
*Her night is illuminated by the light of faith and confidence, as she explains in this same year to Mme. de Sourdon:*

Abandonment—that is what surrenders us to God.
I am quite young, but it seems to me that I have suffered much sometimes.
Oh, then, when everything was dark, when the present was so painful and the future seemed even more gloomy to me, I closed my eyes and abandoned myself like a child in the arms of this Heavenly Father...

We look at ourselves too much, we want to see and understand, we do not have enough confidence in Him who envelops us in His Love.
We must not stop before the cross and regard it in itself, but recollecting ourselves in the light of faith, we must rise higher and think that it is the instrument which is obeying divine Love.
"One thing alone is necessary: Mary has chosen the better part which shall not be taken from her."
This better part, which seems to be my privilege in my beloved solitude of Carmel, is offered by God to every baptized soul.
He offers it to you, dear Madame, in the midst of your cares and maternal concerns.
Believe that His whole desire is to lead you ever deeper into Himself.
Surrender yourself and all your preoccupations to Him...

July 25, 1902, (L 129)

# Daily Work In The Presence of God

156

157

158

159

**156** *The laundry in the basement where they did the wash.*

**157** *Workbasket which they brought to the recreation room, to the cell, and even to the parlor.*

**158** *Elizabeth's cell.*

**159** *Elizabeth's "alpargates" (rope sandals), on the floor of her cell.*

You ask me what my work is in Carmel.
I could answer that for the Carmelite there is only one occupation: "to love, to pray."

June 29, 1903 (L 168)

I wish you could see me at the wash with my habit turned up and splashing the water around. You doubt my ability in this field, and with good reason, but with Jesus I tackle everything and I find everything charming, nothing is difficult or boring.
Ah, how good it is in Carmel; it is the best country in the world, and I can say that I am as happy as a fish in water.

February 11, 1902 (L 108)

When I am not sweeping, I work in our little cell. A straw mattress, a little chair, a board for a desk, and there you have its furnishings, but it is filled with God and I spend such wonderful hours there alone with the Spouse. For me, the cell is something sacred; it is His intimate sanctuary, just for Him and His little bride. We are so happy: "the two of us." I am silent; I listen to Him... it is so good to hear everything He has to say. And I love Him while I ply my needle and work on this dear serge which I have so longed to wear.

June 29, 1903 (L 168)

160

161

162

*The following note which Elizabeth addressed to the one in charge of the "vestry" gives an idea of her humor and her consideration in her relationships with her sisters:*

My dear sister,
I am somewhat confused as to where to place the patch you just gave me.
I left the two sides unsewn until I could be more sure and I would be very grateful if you would come by after mass. Please come in and mark the place, and then look at what I have proposed regarding the front of a habit that is too tight. If you don't like the idea, give me a better one.
You will find pencil and paper on the table in case you have some explanation to give to your little assistant, who loves you and prays for you.

August 1905-March 1906 (L 254)

**160**  *The wooden "sandals" which they wore to go to the garden.
For working in the vegetable garden they put on wooden clogs ("sabots").*

**161-162**  *The "vestry" where Elizabeth helped in the more extensive mending of the garments.*

# He Is Risen!

59a

Oh, if you only knew how beautiful Holy Week is in Carmel!
I wish you could have attended one of our beautiful services, and especially our glorious feast of Easter.
On that day we chant Matins at 3:00 in the morning; we enter choir in procession wearing our white mantles and holding a candle as we sing the Regina Coeli.
At 5:00 A.M. we have the Mass of the Resurrection followed by a magnificent procession in our beautiful garden.
Everything was so still, so mysterious, that it seemed our Master was going to appear to us along the solitary paths as He once appeared to Mary Magdalene. And if our eyes did not see Him, at least our souls met Him in faith.
Faith is so good; it is Heaven in darkness, but one day the veil will fall and we will contemplate Him whom we love in His light. While awaiting the Spouse's "Come," we must spend ourselves, suffer for Him and, above all, love Him greatly.

April 28, 1903 (L 162)

163

**163**  *A pathway in the garden*

Since Our Lord dwells in our souls, His prayer belongs to us.
I wish to communicate with it unceasingly, keeping myself like a
little vase at the Source, at the Fountain of life, so that later I can
communicate Him to souls by letting its floods of infinite
charity overflow.
"I sanctify myself for them so that they may also sanctify
themselves in the truth."

January 25, 1904 (L 191)

**164**  *The northen façade of the monastery and the vegetable garden. On the ground floor, along with other rooms, are the kitchen and the refectory. On the second floor are the cells on the north side—Elizabeth's was on the opposite side overlooking the quadrangle—and the chapter room (the small wing under the bell tower). To the extreme right, the gable of the exterior quarters.*
*As a young girl, Elizabeth could see from her bedroom this northern façade through the trees which bordered the enclosure wall.*

**165**  *A corner of the monastery seen from the garden, located on the western side.*
*The building in the foreground on the left is the infirmary where Elizabeth died.*

**166**  *Recreation in the garden. The photograph, partly out of focus, and taken much later (August 1938), is suggestive of Elizabeth's time.*

**167**  *Well in the garden.*

# Her Wounded Heart Exclaimed, "Here I Am!"

60a

The Carmelite is a given soul,
One immolated for the glory of God.
With her Christ she is crucified;
But how luminous is her calvary!
While gazing on the divine Victim,
A light blazed forth in her soul
And, understanding her sublime mission,
Her wounded heart exclaimed: "Here I am!"

The Carmelite is an adoring soul,
Wholly surrendered to the action of God,
Intently communing through all things,
Her heart uplifted and her eyes full of heaven!
She has found the One Thing Necessary,
The divine Being, Light and Love.
Enfolding the world in her prayer,
She is an apostle in truth.

July 29, 1902 (P 83)

St. John of the Cross says in his Canticle:
> "On the verdant banks
> The turtledove has found
> Its long desired companion!"

Yes, I have found Him whom my soul loves, this One Thing Necessary which no one can take from me. Oh, how good He is! How beautiful He is! I wish to be wholly silent, wholly adoring, so that I may enter into Him ever more deeply and be so filled with Him that I can give Him through prayer to these poor souls who are unaware of the Gift of God.

Oh, won't you please place me in the chalice so that my soul may be wholly bathed in this Blood of my Christ for which I so thirst! May I be wholly pure, wholly transparent so that the Trinity can be reflected in me as in a crystal. It so loves to contemplate its beauty in a soul! This draws it to give itself even more, to come with its favors so that it may effect the great mystery of love and unity!

Ask God that I may live fully my Carmelite life, my life as a bride of Christ; this supposes such a profound union! Why has He loved me so much?

I feel so little, so full of misery, but I love Him; that is all I can do. I love Him with His love; it is a double current between Him who is and her who is not!

August 2, 1902 (L 131)

**168-169** *The double-cloister in front of the oratory, with the entrance door visible.*
*In Elizabeth's time, on a little altar, there was a black wooden statue of "Our Lady of Grace" (photograph 169), honored in the Carmel of Dijon on May 25.*

Saint Teresa says that the soul is like a crystal in which the Divinity is reflected. I so love this comparison, and when I see the sun invade our cloisters with its rays, I think that God invades the soul that seeks only Him in the same way!

Listen to what Saint John of the Cross says: "O soul, most beautiful of creatures, who desire so ardently to know the place where your Beloved dwells in order to seek Him and unite yourself to Him; you yourself are the retreat where He takes refuge, the dwelling where He hides Himself."

That is the whole life of Carmel: to live in Him; then, all sacrifices, all immolations become divine, for through everything the soul sees Him whom it loves and everything leads it to Him; it is a continual heart-to-heart exchange! You see that you can already be a Carmelite in your heart. Love silence and prayer for this is the essence of the life of Carmel. Ask the Queen of Carmel to teach you to adore Jesus in profound recollection...

To Germaine de Gemeaux
September 14, 1902 (L 136)

# Canonical Examination Before Her Profession

57

58

**57-60**  *On December 22, 1902, day of the canonical examination before profession (see General Introduction). In the afternoon, wearing her white veil, the novice left the cloister according to custom and could meet her family in the exterior quarters where these four negatives—which, unfortunately, did not turn out too well—were taken by Georges Chevignard, who married Guite two months before. The differences in the poses are minor. In photograph 58 Guite moved her left hand and only three fingers instead of the four fingers of photograph 57 are visible.*
*In photograph 59, Mme. Catez is now looking at her daughter instead of at the lens. Elizabeth is twenty-two years and five months, Guite is twenty years and ten months, Mme. Catez is fifty-six years and four months.*

59

60

61

Still the afternoon of
December 22, 1902, day of the
canonical examination.
These two photographs, taken
in front of the chapel entrance,
are the work this time of a
Dijon photographer, Mazillier.
The decor has been rapidly
assembled—the edges of the
rug are not flattened out
well—and lack good taste.
The prie-dieu is not in keeping
with the simplicity and poverty
of the Carmelite.
The rug, which serves to hide
the sidewalk in front of the
chapel, does not match the
more sober tiling.
Sister Elizabeth who is
suffering interiorly
(see General Introduction),
must not have felt at ease
in this artificial setting;
it shows in her facial
expression.

62

**61**  *She has on her white mantle,
and a black veil which she was not to
wear officially until January 21,
the day of her veiling, after her profession.
As this black veil was fixed too far back,
the photographer retouched it on the
negative but this clumsy correction
makes Elizabeth's face appear more
somber.*

**62**  *Under the black veil of the professed
can be seen her novice's white veil
sticking out of the scapular in the back.
She is holding her profession crucifix.*

# I Feel My Weakness...

On Epiphany He will make me
His queen, and I will
pronounce the vows that will
unite me to Him forever!
Help me, for I wish to be as
He wants me to be.
I feel my weakness, but He is
in me to prepare me.
A whole life to be spent in
silence, adoration, a heart-to-
heart exchange with the
Spouse!
Pray that I may be faithful;
that I may fulfill His plans for
my soul.

December 29, 1902 (L 149)

*She will write on the very eve
of her profession:*

I have just seen Our Mother
who revealed to me her
uneasiness in seeing me make
my vows in such a state of soul.
Pray for your little one who is
full of anguish.

January 10, 1903 (L 152)

61a

# My Heaven Began In Faith

62a

During the night that preceded the great day, while I was in choir awaiting the Spouse, I understood that my Heaven was beginning on earth—Heaven in faith, with suffering and self-sacrifice for Him whom I love!

July 15, 1903 (L 169)

# Profession, January 11, 1903

On Sunday morning, January 11, 1903, feast of the Epiphany, Sister Elizabeth of the Trinity made her definitive vows (at this time they did not make temporary vows beforehand) of poverty, chastity and obedience before the chapter room altar which was decorated with flowers.
She was surrounded only by her community.
Sister Elizabeth was wholly imbued with the words of Saint Paul: "Offer yourself as a living sacrifice, holy and acceptable to God."
According to custom, she spent the whole day in silence and prayer before celebrating with her sisters during evening recreation.

171

170

172

173

**170**  The crown of flowers which she wore on her profession day.

**171**  The chapter room.

**172**  Father Edmond Vergne, Jesuit, who put Elizabeth at peace the evening before her profession.

**173**  Abbé Jules Courtois, ordinary confessor of the community.

*Light broke through in abundance!*
*Once Elizabeth crossed the threshhold of her definitive*
*commitment by her profession, she fully enjoyed a deep peace,*
*a deep joy in God to whom she continued to surrender herself*
*with absolute fidelity and ardor.*

# Everything Is Beginning!

How many things have happened since my last letter!
I heard the Church say, "Come, Bride of Christ;" she consecrated
me and now all is "consummated." Rather, everything is
beginning, for profession is only a dawn. Each day my "life as
bride" seems to me more beautiful, more luminous, more
enveloped in peace and love.
I so wish to love Him, to love Him as my seraphic Holy Mother
Teresa did, even to dying of it, and that is my whole ambition:
to be the prey of love.

July 15, 1903 (L 169)

**63-66**  *See General Introduction.
The four negatives were taken in the
garden of the monastery around the end
of January-February 1903,
after her veiling.*

# I Have Nothing Else But Him

Who could describe the joy of my soul when, on contemplating the crucifix which I received after my profession and which our Reverend Mother placed "as a seal on my heart," I could say to myself: "At last He is all mine, and I am all His. I have nothing else but him, He is my All!"
And now I have only one desire, to love Him, to love Him all the time, to be zealous for His honor as a true bride, to give Him joy, to make Him happy by preparing a dwelling and a refuge for Him in my soul, so that there He may forget, by the strength of my love, all the abominations of the wicked!

February 15, 1903 (L 156)

# I Am Elizabeth Of The Trinity

64

I am "Elizabeth of the Trinity," that is, Elizabeth disappearing, losing herself, letting herself be possessed by the Three...
Let us join in making our days one continual communion: in the morning let us awake in Love; all day long let us surrender to Love, that is, by doing the will of God, in His presence, with Him, in Him, for Him alone.
Let us give ourselves all the time in the way that He wants. And then, when evening comes, after a dialogue of love which has not ceased in our heart, let us also fall asleep in Love.
Perhaps we will see faults, infidelities; let us abandon them to Love: it is a fire which consumes, so let us make our purgatory in His Love!

August 20, 1903 (L 172)

**64** *Elizabeth, wearing her white mantle, holds her breviary in her hands.*

# How I love This Rule...

I think that in Carmel it is so simple to live by love; from morning to evening the Rule is there to express the will of God moment by moment. If you knew how I love this Rule which is the way in which He wants me to become holy.

I do not know if I will have the happiness of giving to my Spouse the witness of my blood by martyrdom, but at least, if I fully live my Carmelite life, I have the consolation of spending myself for Him, for Him alone.
What difference does the work which He wills for me make. Since He is always with me, prayer, the heart-to-heart exchange, should never end! I feel Him so alive in my soul. I have only to recollect myself to find Him within me, and that is all my happiness.
He has placed within my heart a thirst for the infinite, and such a great need to love, that He alone can satisfy it.
I go to Him, like a little child to its mother, so He may fill, may possess everything, and may take me and carry me away in His arms.
I think that we must be so simple with God!

July 15, 1903 (L 169)

**65** *Elizabeth*

**65a** *Elizabeth holds in her left hand the little volume of the* Rule and Constitutions of the Carmelites.

# To Be The Bride Of Christ!

To be the bride of Christ! "Bride," I must live all that this name
implies of love given and received, of intimacy, of fidelity, of
absolute devotion! To be a bride means to be given as He gave
Himself; it means to be sacrificed as He was, by Him, for Him...
It is Christ making Himself all ours and we becoming "all His!"
To be a bride means to have all rights over His Heart...
It is a heart-to-heart exchange for a whole lifetime...
It is to live with... always with... It means to rest from everything
in Him, and to allow Him to rest from everything in our soul!
It means to know nothing else than to love, to love while adoring,
to love while making reparation, to love while praying, while
asking, while forgetting oneself; to love always in every way!
"To be a bride" means to have eyes only for Him, our thoughts
haunted by Him, our heart wholly taken over, wholly possessed,
as if it had passed out of itself and into Him; our soul filled with His
soul, filled with His prayer, our whole being captivated and given.
It means, by keeping our gaze always fixed on His, to discover His
least sign, His least desire; it means to enter into all His joys,
to share all His sadness. It means to be fruitful, a co-redeemer,
to bring souls to birth in grace, to multiply the adopted children of
the Father, the redeemed of Christ, the co-heirs of His glory.
"To be a bride," a bride of Carmel, means to have the flaming heart
of Elijah, the transpierced heart of Teresa, his "true bride," because
she was zealous for His honor.
Finally, to be taken as bride, a mystical bride, means to have
ravished His Heart to the extent that, forgetting all distance,
the Word pours Himself out in the soul as in the bosom of
the Father with the same ecstasy of infinite love! It is the Father,
the Word and the Spirit possessing the soul, deifying it, consuming
it in the One by love.

1902 (PN 13)

# I Forget No One!

174 *Guite and her husband, Georges Chevignard, during their wedding trip in October 1902.*

175 *Elizabeth often wrote in the evening by the light of her little kerosene lamp, holding her writing case on her knees.*

176 *Mme. de Sourdon, in 1908.*

177 *Yvonne de Rostang, in 1905.*

178 *The young seminarian, André Chevignard, Guite's brother-in-law.*

174

175

God loves you, my Guite;
your union is wholly blessed
by Him!
You will see that both of us
are blessed, each in the way
our Master calls us and wants us
to be!

To her sister Guite on the eve of
her marriage, October 14, 1902
(L 140)

It seems to me that I have
found my Heaven on earth,
since Heaven is God and God
is in my soul.
The day I understood that,
everything became clear to me.
I wish to tell this secret very
softly to those whom I love so
that they also, through
everything, may always cling
to God...

To Mme. de Sourdon, June 1902
(L 122).

Marriage is a vocation also;
how many saints have glorified
God in it...

To Yvonne de Rostang, August
18, 1905 (L 242)

Since we are all members of
one body, inasmuch as we have
an abundance of divine life we
can communicate it in the great
body of the Church.
There are two words which for
me sum up all holiness and all
apostolate: "Union, Love."

To Abbé Chevignard, January
25, 1904 (L 191)

176          177          178

Beloved Mama, if you feel ice forming on your heart, go warm yourself near Him who is a furnace of love and who only creates voids in order to fill them completely!

To her Mother, March 1903 (L 159)

Jesus and Mary loved each other so: all the heart of one flowed into the heart of the other. I am in a good school, beloved Mama! He teaches me to love as He loved, He, the God of all Love.

To her Mother, December 31, 1903 (L 188)

Always love prayer, and when I say prayer, I don't mean so much imposing on oneself a lot of vocal prayers to be recited every day, as that elevation of the soul toward God through all things. This establishes us in a kind of continual communion with the Holy Trinity by quite simply doing everything in their presence.
And a soul united to Jesus is a living smile which radiates Him and which gives Him! Please remember me to Monsieur de Gemeaux. I can still hear his beautiful voice; I so loved our long music sessions!

To Germaine de Gemeaux, December 1905 (L 252)

Oh, my Françoise, you have such an ardent heart; don't you understand what love is when it concerns Him who has so loved us? If only you knew how He loves you, and how I love you also!

To Françoise de Sourdon, November 21, 1903 (L 182)

See, He confides a little angel to you so that you may teach it to know Him and to love Him... That, dear little Mama, is your mission...

To Marie-Louise Maurel, December 15, 1903 (L 186)

Please give my regards to Charles and tell him that his sister in Carmel prays for him every day.

To Mme. Hallo, January 1905 (L 218)

**17a** *Françoise de Sourdon and Elizabeth in 1893. (Photograph 17, page 40)*

**59b** *Mme. Catez, in 1902. (Photograph 59a, page 84)*

**179** *Marie-Louise Maurel, before her marriage.*

**180** *The merry Charles Hallo, during his military service in 1904, playing the role of "Mademoiselle Charlotte!"*

**181** *M. and Mme. de Gemeaux with their children, Germaine (seated in the middle), Yvonne and Albert, in 1908.*

17a

59b

179

180

181

# It Is Through You That God Wants To Be Loved!

**182-184** *Summer 1905.*
*Guite with her husband Georges Chevignard and their children: Sabeth (named for her Carmelite aunt) and Odette (the baby).*
*Guite is twenty-two and a half.*
*Georges is thirty-five.*
*They would have nine children.*
*One of their sons, Pierre, would become a priest.*
*Four daughters would consecrate themselves to the Lord.*
*Sabeth would enter the Carmel of Dijon.*
*As we write these lines, Sister Elizabeth of Jesus is a venerable octogenarian.*

Oh, if you knew how He loves you and how, through you, He wants to be loved by your little angels!

To her sister Guite, July 3, 1905 (L 233)

*On August 13, 1905, Elizabeth writes to Guite (L 239):*

I have just been reading in Saint Paul some splendid things on the mystery of the divine adoption.
Naturally, I thought of you—it would have been quite extraordinary if I hadn't: you who are a mother and who know what depths of love God has placed in your heart for your children, you can grasp the grandeur of this mystery; to be children of God, my Guite, doesn't that thrill you? Through everything, in the midst of your maternal cares, while you give yourself to your little angels, you can retire into this house of our Father, in "the center of our souls," in order to surrender yourself to the Holy Spirit so that He may transform you in God, and may imprint in your soul the Image of the divine Beauty, so that the Father, lovingly bending over you, may see only His Christ...

182

*Perhaps already having a premonition of her death, Elizabeth writes a letter (L 240) in August 1905 to her little nieces so that they might read it later.*
*Elizabeth was very aware of the presence of the Trinity in every baptized person:*

To those who gaze on you in your mama's arms, you seem very small, but your fond aunt who looks at you in the light of faith sees in you a nature of infinite grandeur: for from all eternity God "has carried you in His thought; He has predestined you to be conformed to the image of His Son Jesus, and by holy baptism He has clothed you with Himself, thus making you His children, and at the same time His living temple" (St. Paul). O dear little sanctuaries of Love, when I see the splendor that radiates in you, and yet which is only the dawn, I fall silent and adore Him who creates such marvels!

*But Elizabeth makes quite another commentary of the photographs:*

Sabeth looks so sweet with her dolls, and with her hand in her mouth.
She has inherited her dear mama's habit!
The group picture of the little ones is so charming.
Sabeth has a protective little air for Odette which reminds me of her Carmelite aunt who so loved to play the big sister with her little Guite.
On seeing how she has filled out, I can hardly believe that this is the thin little girl whose blouses I had to pad!

To her mother
September 17, 1905 (L 243)

183

184

# Within Me I Have The Prayer Of Jesus Christ

"House of God," I have within me the prayer
Of Jesus Christ, the divine adorer,
It takes me to souls and to the Father,
As that is its double movement.
> To be savior with my Master,
> That is also my mission.
> So I must disappear,
> Lose myself in Him through union.
>> Jesus, Word of life,
>> United to You forever,
>> Your virgin and Your victim
>> Will radiate Your love:
>> "Amo Christum."

Mother of the Word, oh tell me your mystery.
After the moment of the Incarnation,
Tell me how you spent your life
Buried in adoration.
> In a peace wholly ineffable,
> A mysterious silence,
> You entered the Unfathomable Being,
> Bearing within you "the gift of God."
>> Oh, keep me always
>> In the divine embrace.
>> May I bear the imprint
>> Of this God of all Love:
>> "Amo Christum."

December 25, 1903 (P 88)

66a

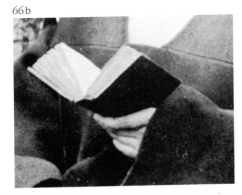

66b

His charity, His "exceeding
charity," to use St. Paul's words,
that is my vision on earth.
Will we ever understand how
much we are loved?
I think that this is indeed
the knowledge of the saints.
In his magnificent epistles
St. Paul preaches nothing else
but this mystery of the love
of Christ...
Let us unite in order to make
Him forget everything by
the strength of our love,
and let us be, as St. Paul says,
"the praise of His glory."

January 25, 1904 (L 191)

I enjoy pondering St. Paul's
letters.

June 1, 1905 (L 230)

**66**  *The last of the four photographs
taken at the end of January-beginning
of March, 1903.
The negative is damaged; it is warped at
Elizabeth's left cheek.
In her left hand the Carmelite is holding
her* Christian's Manual, *open at
the New Testament.
There is a little bandage on the
index finger.*

66

# O My God, Trinity Whom I Adore

O my God,
Trinity whom I adore,
help me to forget myself entirely
that I may be established in You
as still and as peaceful
as if my soul were already in eternity.
May nothing trouble my peace
or make me leave You,
O my Unchanging One,
but may each minute
carry me further
into the depths of Your Mystery.
Give peace to my soul;
make it Your heaven,
Your beloved dwelling
and Your resting place.
May I never leave You there alone
but be wholly present,
my faith wholly vigilant,
wholly adoring,
and wholly surrendered
to Your creative Action.

O my beloved Christ,
crucified by love,
I wish to be a bride
for Your Heart;
I wish to cover You with glory;
I wish to love You...
even to dying of it!
But I feel my weakness,
and I ask You
to "clothe me with Yourself,"
to identify my soul
with all the movements of Your Soul,
to overwhelm me,
to possess me,
to substitute Yourself for me
that my life may be
but a radiance of Your Life.
Come into me as Adorer,
as Restorer,
as Savior.

**185** *This Christ is not a work of art, but it is Sister Elizabeth's own crucifix which she had before her eyes or on her heart when writing these lines. It is the one which she would kiss a few days before her death while saying: "We have loved each other so much!"*

O Eternal Word,
Word of my God,
I want to spend my life
in listening to You,
to become wholly teachable
that I may learn all from You.
Then, through all nights,
all voids,
all helplessness,
I want to gaze on You always
and remain in Your great light.
O my beloved Star,
so fascinate me
that I may not withdraw
from Your radiance.

O consuming Fire,
Spirit of Love,
"come upon me,"
and create in my soul
a kind of incarnation of the Word:
that I may be
another humanity for Him
in which He can renew His whole Mystery.
And You, O Father,
bend lovingly
over Your poor little creature;
"cover her with Your shadow,"
seeing in her
only the "Beloved
in whom You are well pleased."

O my Three,
my All,
my Beatitude,
infinite Solitude,
Immensity in which I lose myself,
I surrender myself to You
as Your prey.
Bury Yourself in me
that I may bury myself in You
until I depart to contemplate
in Your light
the abyss of Your greatness.

November 21, 1904 (PN 15)

# The Autograph Text of "O My God, Trinity Whom I Adore."

**186-187** *This text—on a very thin sheet—torn from a notebook and written on both sides—is reproduced here in the original format: 14.1 x 9.3 cm.*

*Elizabeth made several spelling mistakes, for example, the word "oubliez" in the second line.*

# He Hollows Out Abysses In My Soul

During the great silence,
in choir quite close to Him,
I loved to say to myself:
"He is my All, my one
and only All."
What happiness, what peace
that gives to the soul.
He is the only one;
I have given Him all.
If I look at it from an earthly
point of view, I see the solitude,
and even the emptiness, for I
cannot say that my heart has
not suffered; but if my gaze
remains always fixed on Him,
my luminous Star, oh, then all
the rest disappears and I lose
myself in Him like a drop of
water in the Ocean!
It is all calm, all peaceful,
and the peace of God is so
good; that is what St. Paul
speaks of when he says that it
"exceeds all understanding."
I have such a hunger for Him;
He hollows out abysses in my
soul, abysses which He alone
can fill.
To do that He leads me into
deep silence which I no longer
wish to leave.

January 4, 1904 (L 190)

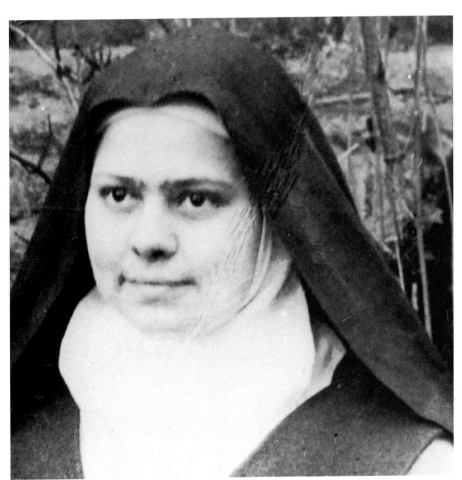
66c

*Still so young, Elizabeth is already at the evening of her life.*
*She feels her illness—Addison's disease, incurable at that time—*
*taking its course of destruction in her. Her earthly journey is*
*coming to an end, the sun is setting, but her invisible Guests, the*
*"Three" whom she so loves, will never abandon her...*

# ... Drained In My Whole Being...

188

189

**188**  *The stairway which leads to the cell corridor.*

**189**  *The cell corridor. Elizabeth's cell is at the end of the corridor, on the right.*

In the morning, after the recitation of the Little Hours,
I already felt at the end of my strength and wondered how I
could make it to evening. When mother prioress let me rest,
I felt no relief; drained in my whole being, I found neither a
comfortable position nor deep sleep, so that I could not have
said whether day or night brought more exhaustion.
Prayer was still the best remedy for my pain.
I spent the time of the great silence in a real agony which I
united to that of my divine Master, staying close to Him by the
choir grille. It was an hour of pure suffering but it obtained for
me the strength to say Matins; I then had a certain ease in
concentrating on God. Afterwards, my weakness returned, and
thanks to the darkness, I reached our cell as best I could without
being noticed, often leaning against the wall.
(S 172-173).

# I Was So Happy To Think I Would Die A Carmelite...

**67** *April 1906.*
*Elizabeth is twenty-five years and nine months.*
*As her death seemed imminent, this photograph would be a last consolation for her family, a last visit that Elizabeth would make to them.*
*Above her head can be seen the print that Mme. de Sourdon gave her (see L 246), representing the Annunciation.*
*Her large black veil has been placed on her for the occasion.*

*Moved to the infirmary in the last days of March 1906, Elizabeth almost died in a serious attack which she herself recalls:*

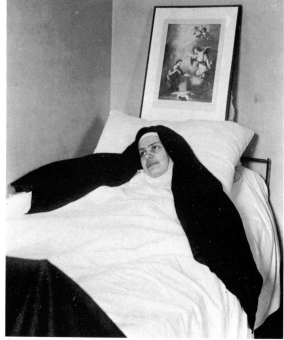
67

On the evening of Palm Sunday, I had a very severe attack and I thought the hour had finally arrived when I was going to fly away to the infinite realms to contemplate unveiled this Trinity which has already been my dwelling here below.
In the calm and silence of this night, I received Extreme Unction and the visit of my Master.
It seemed to me that He was awaiting this moment to break my bonds.
Oh! my little sister, what ineffable days I spent expecting the great vision and in my desire to go to Him I felt that He delayed in coming.
I was so happy to think I would die a Carmelite...

June 10, 1906 (L 278)

# To Share Fully
# In The Passion of Christ

The soul that wants to serve
God day and night must be
resolved to share *fully* in
its Master's passion.
It is one of the redeemed
who in its turn must redeem
other souls.
"I suffer in my body what is
lacking in the passion of Christ
for the sake of His body,
which is the Church."
She walks the way of Calvary at
the right of her crucified,
annihilated, humiliated King as
He goes to His passion
"to make the glory of His
grace blaze forth."
He wants to associate His bride
in His work of redemption and
this sorrowful way which she
follows seems like the path of
Beatitude to her, not only
because it leads there but also
because her holy Master makes
her realize that she must go
beyond the bitterness in
suffering to find in it,
as He did, her rest.

Last Retreat 13

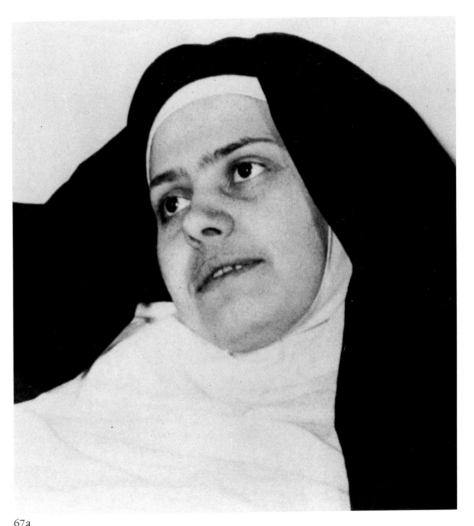

67a

*The vineyards of the Burgundian "Côte d'Or." At Meursault. The Abbé Chevignard was assistant pastor there in 1904. Elizabeth supported his apostolic work by her prayer and the offering of her Carmelite life. She wrote him: "I am not forgetting that I am the assistant of the assistant of Meursault." (L 250)*

O Love, Love!
You know how I love You, how I desire
to contemplate You!
You know also how I suffer...
And yet, thirty, forty years more if You like,
I am ready.
Consume my whole substance for Your glory.
Let it be distilled
drop by drop
for Your Church.

# In The Infirmary

*The two windows closest to the corner of the building are those of her infirmary cell (on the second floor, above the cloister) where she would live this last phase of her life and where she would die. Behind the double windows of the next wing, above the oratory, are two infirmary rooms that Elizabeth would often walk through during her illness (from the end of the month of July, after having been bed-ridden for more than three months) in order to go to the little "tribune" (photograph 191) whose grille overlooked the chapel. Although photograph 192—restored after Elizabeth's death—lacks clarity, it allows us to see the infirmary cell as she knew it: on the left, the ceramic stove, a chair, the window which looks out over a terrace above the cloister, a little table with her breviary and her crucifix, a statue of Our Lady of Lourdes (which belonged to Elizabeth when she was a young girl and which her mother brought to the invalid), above, a picture of Jesus on the cross, and, lastly, an arm chair and the corner of her bed.*

I am God's little recluse, and when I return to my dear cell to continue there the conversation begun at the tribune, a divine joy takes hold of me; I so love solitude with Him alone, and I lead a simple hermit's life that is truly delightful.
You know, it is far from being exempt from helplessness; I, too, need to seek my Master who hides Himself; but then I arouse my faith, and I am happier at not enjoying His presence in order to make Him enjoy my love.
At night, when you awake, unite yourself to me.
I wish I could invite you here near me; it is so mysterious, so silent, this little cell with its white walls clearly marked by a black cross without the Corpus. It is for me where I must immolate myself at every moment in order to be conformed to my crucified Spouse.

To her sister Guite
July 16, 1906, (L 298)

190

191

192

193

I seem to feel myself being
destroyed...
Sometimes it is painful for
nature and I can assure you that
if I were to remain at that level,
I would feel only my cowardice
in the face of suffering.
But that is looking at things
from the human point of view!
Very quickly I open the eye of
my soul in the light of faith.
And this faith tells me that it is
love who is slowly consuming
me; then I feel a tremendous
joy...
The Greatness Of Our
Vocation, 7

**193-195** *Elizabeth's view of the
quadrangle from her cell
(photographs taken in 1978).
But the large cross (photograph 193)
which had no Corpus in her time,
is taken from the oratory beneath
the infirmary.
On the second floor, the next to last
window of the left wing is that of the cell
she occupied before her illness.
Photograph 195: her bed in the infirmary
cell where she died.*

194

195

Neither trials from without nor from within can make her leave
the fortress in which her Master has enclosed her.
She no longer feels "hunger or thirst," for in spite of her
consuming desire for Beatitude, she is satisfied by this food
which was her Master's: "The will of the Father."
She no longer suffers from suffering. Then the Lamb can "lead her
to the fountain of life," where He wills, as He wills, for she does
not look at the paths on which she is walking, she simply gazes at
the Shepherd who is leading her.

Last Retreat, 14

"In my own flesh I fill up what is lacking in the passion of Jesus
Christ for the sake of His body, which is the Church"; the apostle
finds his happiness in this! The thought pursues me...

The Greatness of our Vocation, 7

# In Heaven I Will Not Forget You!

196

197

198

199

200

A Dieu, beloved Françoise,
I cannot go on.
And in the silence of our
rendezvous you will guess,
you will understand, what I do
not tell you.
I send you a kiss.
I love you as a mother loves
her little child.
A Dieu, my little one...

To Françoise de Sourdon,
September 1906 (L 310)

I am so weak that I can hardly
hold a pencil, and yet I need to
thank you from my heart which
is so deeply moved by your
delicate thoughtfulness.
I award you the diploma of
confectioner: your chocolates
are so good!
Thank you a thousand times!
I do not forget you on my cross
where I taste unknown joys...

To Anne-Marie d'Avout
October 1906 (L 328a)

Dear Mama, whom I love, you
fill your child's plates so well
that you do not need to send
her any cheese after mass...

To sister Marthe of Jesus,
in 1906 (L 281)

Before I die I dream of being
transformed into Jesus crucified
and that gives me so much
strength in my suffering...
Dear sister, we should have no
other ideal than to conform to
this divine Model; then what
fervor we would bring to
sacrifice, to contempt of
ourselves, if we always had
the eyes of our heart turned
toward Him.
How happy I was at Albert's
great success...
Tell your dear parents that in
Heaven I will not forget them
nor dear Yvonne either.

To Germaine de Gemeaux,
October 1906 (L 324)

Ah, in my Father's House
I will not forget
Your most delicate care,
your tender love.
For me, God has given you
the goodness of a mother,
And I love you, O my sister,
with the heart of a child.

To Sister Anne of Jesus,
July 1906 (P 104)

There is a Being who is Love and who wishes that we live in communion with Him. Oh Mama, this is delightful. He is there keeping me company, helping me to suffer, urging me to go beyond my suffering to rest in Him.

To her mother,
October 1906 (L 327)

Your little praise of glory cannot sleep; she suffers very much; but in her soul, although the anguish penetrates there too, she feels such peace... I feel my Three so close to me; I am more overwhelmed by happiness than by pain. My Master has reminded me that I am not to choose my sufferings, so I plunge with Him into immense pain with much fear and anguish.

To Mother Germaine,
October 1906 (L 320)

I pray and sacrifice myself for your little Jaja.
Who knows if God is not waiting for me to go to Heaven in order to arrange her future with the Blessed Virgin?

To Mme. Gout de Bize,
October 1906 (L 330)

*Here is an excerpt from her very last letter, adressed to Charles Hallo. Elizabeth dictated it just a few days before her death:*

My dear brother, before going to Heaven your Elizabeth wants to tell you once more of her deep affection for you and her plan to help you, day by day, until you join her in Heaven. Call your little sister; in this way you will increase her happiness in Heaven. I no longer have strength to dictate these last wishes of a very loving sister. When I am close to God, recollect yourself in prayer and we will meet each other in an even deeper way. I leave you a medal from my rosary; wear it always in memory of your Elizabeth who will love you even more in Heaven.

November 1906 (L 342)

201  *Mme. Catez and Guite (around 1902) on the balcony of their home.*

202-203  *Mme. Berthe Gout de Bize and her daughter Jaja.*

147a  *Mother Germaine, in 1908 (Photograph 147, page 73)*

204  *Charles Hallo, in 1906.*

202

203

147a

201

204

**68**   *Last photograph of Elizabeth
when she was alive.
It is taken on the terrace near
the infirmary (on the left):
on the right can be seen the arch of
a choir window.
Elizabeth is wearing the lighter habit
that she received on October 4th,
so it is probably only a little after this
date, about a month before her death.
At her side is the statue of Our Lady of
Lourdes which she called from then on
"Janua Coeli" (Gate of Heaven).
She is holding in her right hand
the rosary which she received from
her friend Antoinette de Bobet
(see L 261).
In her lap is a book containing
"The Spiritual Canticle"
and "The Living Flame" of
St. John of the Cross.
Although quite weak, Elizabeth still tries
to sit very straight.
Though the negative is not very sharp
it allows us to see how thin and
emaciated her face has become compared
to photograph 67 of April.
One can see the rings under her eyes.
Her hand is already very wasted,
the fingers bony.
One month later, on her death bed,
her face would be frightfully thin.
She is twenty-six years and almost
three months...*

# I Will Keep My Strength For You!

To keep one's strength for the Lord is to unify one's whole being by means of interior silence, to collect all one's powers in order to employ them in the one work of love.
A soul that debates with its self, that is taken up with its feelings and pursues useless thoughts and desires, scatters its forces, for it is not wholly directed toward God. Its lyre does not vibrate in unison and when the master plays it, He cannot draw from it divine harmonies, for it is still too human and discordant.

Last Retreat, 3

A praise of glory is a soul of silence that remains like a lyre under the mysterious touch of the Holy Spirit so that He may draw from it divine harmonies...

Heaven in Faith, 43

**16a** *Elizabeth's hands as a young pianist. (see page 38)*

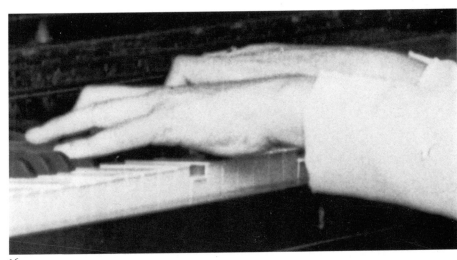

16a

# The Queen Of Martyrs

After Jesus Christ, doubtless at the distance that there is between the Infinite and the finite, there is one who was also the great praise of glory of the Holy Trinity...

Her humility was so real for she was always forgetful, unaware, freed from self...

This Queen of virgins is also Queen of martyrs.

Oh! How beautiful she is to contemplate during her long martyrdom, so serene, enveloped in a kind of majesty that radiates both strength and gentleness...

She is there at the foot of the cross, standing, full of strength and courage, and here my Master says to me: "Behold your Mother."

He gives her to me for my Mother... And now that He has returned to the Father and has substituted me for Himself on the cross so that "I may suffer in my body what is lacking in His passion for the sake of His body, which is the Church," the Blessed Virgin is again there to teach me to suffer as He did, to tell me, to make me hear those last songs of His soul which no one else but she, His Mother, could overhear.

When I shall have said: "All is consummated," it is again she, "Gate of Heaven," who will lead me into the heavenly courts...

Last Retreat, 40-41

# In The Evening Of Life Love Alone Remains

In the light of eternity the soul sees things as they really are.
Oh, how empty is all that has not been done for God and with God!
I beg you, oh, mark everything with the seal of love!
It alone endures. How serious life is: each minute is given us in order to "root" us deeper in God, as St. Paul says, so that the resemblance to our divine Model may be more striking, the union more intimate. But to realize this plan which is that of God Himself, here is the secret: forget self, give up self, ignore self, look at the Master, look only at Him, receive as coming directly from His love both joy and suffering; this places the soul on such serene heights!
I leave you my faith in the presence of God, of the God who is all Love dwelling in our souls. I confide to you: it is this intimacy with Him "within" which has been the beautiful sun illuminating my life, making it already an anticipated Heaven; it is what sustains me today in my suffering. I do not fear my weakness; it is that which gives me confidence. For the Strong One is within me and His power is all-mighty. He is able to do, says the Apostle, abundantly more than we can hope for.

End of October 1906, (L 333)

*A few days before her death Elizabeth said to her sisters:*

Everything passes! In the evening of life love alone remains...

# Consumed, Ravaged By Illness...
# Consummated In Love...

69

70

**69-70** *Elizabeth on her deathbed in the infirmary parlor. Probably shocked by the frightful appearance of the dead nun (photograph 69), the sisters attempted to close the eyelids more (photograph 70).*

# Elizabeth Dies At Dawn On November 9, 1906

I am going to Light,
to Love,
to Life!

*(Her last words)*

I think that in Heaven
my mission will be to draw souls
by helping them to go out of themselves
in order to cling to God
by a wholly simple and loving movement,
and to keep them
in this great silence within
which will allow God
to communicate Himself to them
and to transform them into Himself.

October 28, 1906 (L 335)

**Glory to God**
in the highest
and peace
to his people on earth.
We praise you,
We bless you,
We adore you,
We glorify you,
We give you thanks
**For your great glory.**

# Index

This list cites excerpts from the *Complete Works* of Blessed Elizabeth of the Trinity. The Roman numerals in parentheses refer to the volumes in which they are found. Volumes II and III are in preparation.